PARENTING

Guide to Toilet Training

PARENTING

Guide to
Toilet Training

With a Story for You and Your Child to Share

by Anne Krueger
with the Editors of
PARENTING magazine

BALLANTINE BOOKS
NEW YORK

For Halley and Gracie

A Ballantine Book
The Random House Publishing Group

Copyright © 2001 by PARENTING magazine

All rights reserved under International and Pan-American Copyright Conventions. Published in the United States by The Random House Publishing Group, a division of Random House, Inc., New York, and simultaneously in Canada by Random House of Canada Limited, Toronto.

Ballantine and colophon are registered trademarks of Random House, Inc.

www.ballantinebooks.com

LIBRARY OF CONGRESS CATALOGING-IN-PUBLICATION DATA
Krueger, Anne.
    Parenting guide to toilet training: story for you and your child to share / Anne Krueger; the editors of Parenting magazine.—1st American ed.
        p. cm.
    Includes index.
    ISBN 0-345-41182-X
    1. Toilet training. 2. Parenting. I. Parenting magazine. II. Title.

HQ770.5 .K78 2001
649'.62—dc21   00-067423

Text design by Michaelis/Carpelis Design Associates, Inc.
Cover photo by Ericka McConnell
Illustrations by Mary Lynn Blasutta

Manufactured in the United States of America

First Edition: April 2001

10 9 8 7 6 5 4

Contents

Contents

Contents

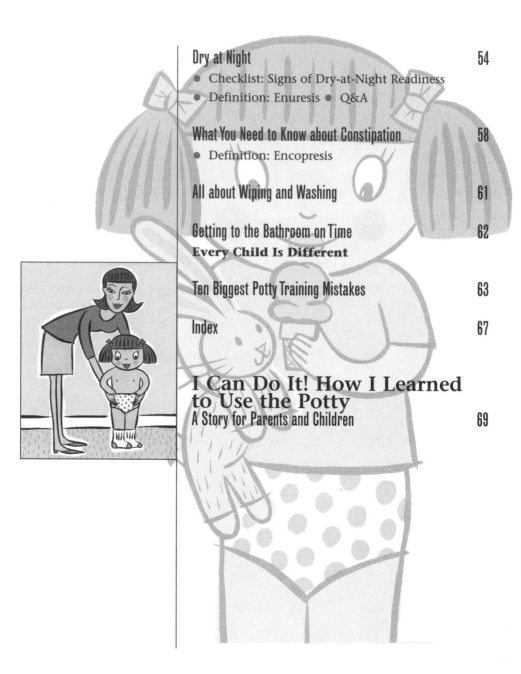

Acknowledgments

Like the process of toilet training, writing a book can be either a struggle or a breeze—depending upon the attitude of the parties involved. Thanks to the relaxed and inspiring environment created by PARENTING franchise development editor Bruce Raskin and editorial director Janet Chan, this book has been a joy to create. And thanks to photo editor Lisa Hilgers and illustrator Mary Lynn Blasutta, it's a pleasure to look at.

I also have to thank my daughters, Halley Rose and Emily Grace, for letting me tell tales about their potty training adventures and for test-driving the children's story "I Can Do It! How I Learned to Use the Potty." And Gracie, thanks for letting me borrow "Bun Bun."

A.K.

Introduction

Your child hits a certain magical age and suddenly visions start filling your head: You see yourself taking a short road trip without a diaper bag. You look in the closet and there seems to be two cubic feet of extra space (no diapers!). Your child suddenly looks several pounds slimmer (no diapers!). Your wallet is fatter (no diapers!).

Yes, all those wonderful things will happen, but potty training won't occur on a particular magical date or at a certain magical age. It won't happen overnight. It may not even take place all in one year. But it will—eventually—happen.

How and when potty training happens has become a major debate among medical professionals and parents, spurred on in part by the introduction of extra-large diapers. There is the "wait until the child is ready" school versus the more extreme "train 'em by the time they're two" school.

Parents can, to some extent, control *how* potty training happens, but not *when*. Get used to that idea right now. Your child is in charge of the when. Most children begin to show signs of readiness between twenty and thirty months of age. Wait for those signs. You'll have to use all of your willpower to control your urge to hurry your child up, but there are excellent reasons not to rush. Consider this: Just as the person on his deathbed rarely says "I wish I'd spent more time at the office," few parents with potty trained children look back and wish they'd started sooner. Most say, "We should have worried less and started later," or "I wish we'd been more relaxed about potty training." They've learned from experience that starting their child earlier doesn't mean he'll finish sooner. They've learned that a relaxed approach to teaching a child how to use the potty is best.

Relax. It's a word that comes up often when experts talk about successful potty training, and it's a word that appears repeatedly in this book. Parents, be relaxed. Take a relaxed approach to teaching. Don't worry. Being relaxed is one of the surefire things you can do to increase your child's odds of a stress-free transition from diapers to the potty. If you only take one thing away with you after reading this book, we hope it's the *R* word. But how, exactly, do you relax?

In order to do so, you need to know and understand the following:

- how a child's body and mind work
- how to recognize signs of readiness
- how to talk effectively about potty training with your child
- how to choose a training option that's best for your family
- when and how to start
- what problems and setbacks to expect
- how your own potty training past colors how you feel about the task at hand

To give parents what they need to relax, the PARENTING *Guide to Potty Training* is divided into five parts.

Get Ready   Review your own attitudes about potty training and think about what kind of teacher you will be; learn how your child's body works and how to recognize when he's ready to use the potty.

Get Set   Prepare for the real thing. Comparison shop for potties, stock up on supplies and easy-on and easy-off clothing. Make sure you and your caregiver or daycare provider agree on potty training techniques.

Go!   A three-step plan (telling, showing, trying) that will get you and your child started; the eight stages of potty practice; plus, how to praise, the pros and cons of rewards, and more.

Keep Going   Dealing with setbacks and challenges, surviving the public rest room, making the transition to night dryness, and how to avoid the most common potty training mistakes.

I Can Do It!   A children's story that gives kids the skills necessary to be a potty training success.

Teaching (learning) should always precede training (doing). That's why half of this book is about preparing yourself and your child for the potty. As my daughter learned in a third-grade lesson about study habits, *PPPPP.* Prior Planning Prevents Poor Performance. It's no more true and important than during this first parent-child collaboration called potty training. Learn all you can about yourself and your child before you begin, follow her cues and your Prior Planning will Produce Peak Performance. If you have faith in yourself and your child, before you know it your "dream" of no more diapers *will* come true.

Anne Krueger
with the Editors of PARENTING

PARENTING

Guide to
Toilet Training

CHAPTER ONE

Get Ready

Before you do even a smidgen of talking about the potty with your child, read this chapter. Besides learning to relax, which is critical, there are two other things that will greatly increase your odds of toilet training success: Know thyself and know thy child. This chapter is aimed at helping you increase your awareness of both.

The whole idea of potty training makes many parents nervous and it's important to know why and to decide what kind of teacher you want to be—before training starts. It's also essential to understand your child's anatomy and how his mind and body work so that you can help him manage this learning process. Understanding your child's strengths and limitations will help you avoid the traps of rushing him or introducing him to the potty before he's ready. Don't despair, he *will* show you when he's ready—usually between twenty and thirty months of age.

Understanding Yourself

It's safe to say that most parents don't approach the task of toilet training with leaps and squeals of joy. What is it about toilet training that gets parents' own panties in such a bundle?

Why You Are the Way You Are

As a society we're squeamish about our bodies and about bodily functions. Going to the toilet isn't something most of us really want to talk about. It doesn't help that the body parts involved in urinating and defecating double as, or are near, our sexual organs. As a result, we're doubly squeamish.

Second, we're the products of our past. Many of us were trained too early and that's left us with some vague negative feelings. We may have parents who have told us so many times that *we* were trained in the "good old days," when children went to the potty on their own well before age two (see Flashback: The History of Toilet Training on page 6), that we feel like parental potty training failures before we've even started.

Third, we're products of the present. As a society we've graduated beyond trying to have a child toilet trained by age one, but we still seem to obsess over it. When a child uses the potty has become a major milestone—like baby's first step—that is greatly anticipated, worried over, celebrated. More than that, how soon or how easily your child is trained seems to have become a reflection on your parenting skills or a measure of your child's intelligence.

Add to that the fact that urinating and defecating into a toilet are so routine to parents that they've forgotten what a complex learning process is involved. Many parents don't know the first thing about how to start telling their child about using the toilet. No wonder we're anxious.

DEFINITION
Toilet Training

This term is used throughout the book. Some experts have discarded the phrase in favor of the more politically correct *toilet learning*, which they believe better supports the notion that the child needs to learn at his own pace and not be arbitrarily trained at a certain time or in a certain way.

We agree with the theory but prefer to avoid a semantics muddle. When we use *toilet training* we are not referring to some sort of boot camp but to a gentle process by which parent and child work together to achieve potty training. In fact, in most toilet training situations, the parent is being trained just as much as the child.

What Kind of Teacher Are You?

It's often been said that patience is a virtue. And so it is when it comes to teaching your child to use the potty. But being patient doesn't come naturally to everyone. It's helpful for parents to think about their own temperament and their parenting style before they embark upon toilet training. Your child will sense when you're impatient or unhappy with her or her performance. Losing your cool can undermine all of your good intentions and efforts.

If you're not a particularly patient person, think in advance about how you'll handle certain situations that are bound to arise—for example, the fifth time your child says he absolutely must go to the potty but screams and cries and goes in his pants when he gets there. Or how about the tenth time your child says she doesn't have to use the potty and then gets in the car and—voila—within three minutes she has to go *right now*. At times like this, some parents find that it's helpful to have a little mantra that they chant to calm themselves down: "patience is a virtue, patience is a virtue. . . ." Others decide that one parent will handle one part of potty training and the more patient parent will handle the hot-button aspects, such as the inevitable accidents.

If you're a control freak, you may also have a frustrating time teaching your child. And he'll be frustrated, too. How can he feel pride in his own achievements if you're doing everything for him? If you're really overbearing, he'll rebel and decide this isn't something he wants to do right now. No amount of cajoling or threatening on your part can change his decision. Parents need to be willing to let their child succeed or fail his own way, in his own time.

It's equally important to recognize that a child's inability to get to the potty on time isn't willful disobedience. It's an accident. Toilet training shouldn't be used as a form of discipline, and accidents shouldn't be punished.

Of course, there's the opposite end of the teaching-style spectrum. In an overreaction to potty training zealots, some parents decide to take a complete hands-off approach. "He'll train when he's good and ready," a friend of mine told me recently. That's very true. But that doesn't mean a parent should take a total laissez-faire attitude. There's a big difference between not pushing and setting up no parameters whatsoever. Toddlers need to know what's expected of them; then they can succeed on their own timetable.

FLASHBACK
The History of Potty Training

Potty training philosophy has gone through an amazing change during the twentieth century.

1900

At the beginning of the century, parents started training their child as early as possible, sometimes as early as the first month. The goal of the training was to force the child to relieve himself at a particular time. To achieve this, mothers used a variety of approved methods, including enemas or suppositories. The mother then spent long periods of time with a pot under the child's bottom, waiting for results.

Back then, the notion that the child needed to learn at his own pace would have been laughable. The pace was mostly determined by the lack of indoor plumbing (no hot water, no washing machines). One less month of diaper washing was quite an incentive.

1920s

A child with "a mind of her own" wouldn't have been popular in the early 1900s. Children were viewed as extensions of the parents, and the parents were very much in charge. It wasn't uncommon for a six-month-old child to be tied to a potty chair until she "did" what she was told: produced a BM. Noncompliance was considered to be a very bad form of disobedience.

If your parents or grandparents were trained during this era, you can begin to understand where their rigid views of toilet training come from.

1950s

By the middle of the century, the toilet training timetable had eased a bit, perhaps because of improvements in plumbing or because of more knowledge about the subject.

When I was being trained in the late 1950s, it was routine for a mom to "pot" her child whenever she looked as if she might have to urinate or defecate. In reality, it was the mother who was being trained. It became her job to identify a child's "gotta go" signals and get the child on the potty in time. For the child, who was usually around eight to eighteen months of age, having a bowel movement or urinating while actually on the potty was hit or miss. Their bodily functions were still mostly involuntary and out of their control.

1980s

Experts and parents recognize that a child must be ready before potty training can begin and that learning to use the toilet is the child's achievement, not something a parent can force the child to do.

Understanding Your Child

Knowing yourself and understanding your own attitudes toward potty training is half the battle. Understanding what's going on inside your child's mind and body is the other half.

Many parents become quite frustrated with potty training because they believe they've explained to their child what's to be done, have even demonstrated the skill, and their toddler still seems clueless. Is he a slow learner? Is he disobeying the parent on purpose?

Probably neither of the above. Most likely the child simply isn't ready to learn about the potty. He hasn't matured enough physically or emotionally. Or he doesn't understand what's expected of him (see A Three-Step Potty Plan, page 32). Moving from diapers to going on the toilet, after all, is not simple. It's a very big deal.

Babies, for instance, don't even have a concept of wet and dry. As they mature, they gain a sense of what is and isn't comfortable. Eventually they figure out their discomfort is caused by something that is wet or mushy in their diaper.

During their first year, maybe longer, they have no names for what's in their diaper and no notion that their own body is producing the stuff. Another year will go by before most children can make the connection between how their body feels and the act of defecating or urinating. There's a world of difference (and usually several months) between a child understanding "Hey, there's something in my pants" and "I'm going poo right now!" Even more body awareness and control is required before that child will be able to understand "Ohhh, I gotta go."

How Children Develop Bladder and Bowel Control

There's a perfectly logical sequence to how children master bladder and bowel control. Knowing the chronology can help you gauge your child's progress.

Nighttime Bowel Control

As they mature, children's eating habits become more regular, and so do their bowel movements. Often they develop nighttime bowel control between ages one and two. What a pleasant surprise it is to change the morning diaper and not have it filled with hours-old BM. It's a good feeling for the child, too, but she's probably unaware that something momentous has happened. It's mostly an involuntary behavior.

Daytime Bowel Control

Because the physical sensations of passing a bowel movement are so much more intense than urinating, toddlers usually recognize that they've made a BM before they understand that they've wet their diaper. To learn to control their bowels and get to the potty in time, a toddler has to go through the following past/present/future stages:

- Be aware that he has had a bowel movement (the past).
- Understand when he's in the process of having a BM (the present).
- Recognize the cues that signal he may *soon* have to have a bowel movement, that is, a feeling of fullness or of pressure, the urge to squat or push or strain (the future).

Toddlers show their awareness that they've had a BM in many ways—by crying, pointing at their diaper, or trying to pull it off. Later, they may indicate they're going to the bathroom by squatting or grunting as they fill their pants.

From there, it's quite a big leap to being able to anticipate a bowel movement. (To help your child understand the feelings that indicate a full bladder or pending bowel movement, see "I Can Do It!," page 68.)

If your toddler is fairly regular, he may deliver a BM into the potty every morning like clockwork if you put him there. If his schedule is disrupted, though, he's likely to go in his pants. He's not really making the connection between "I'm sitting here on the potty" and "I feel the need to make a poopoo" (or vice versa). It's more a matter of chance that he's in the right place at the right time.

You could call this potty training, but the only one really being trained in this case is you. Like previous generations who prided themselves on their skillful early training, it's really *you* anticipating when your child needs to get to the potty and you putting him there. It's hard for your child to feel great pride in the well-placed BM since he's not sure what he did. He'll eventually catch on that the potty is where the BM goes, but he'll still need to learn to read his body's signals before he can be in control.

Some children hold in their bowel movements. Many parents are surprised by this behavior, but it's not uncommon. It may be a reaction to overzealous potty training or just a reluctance to pass a bowel movement into the potty. Because this can become a bad habit and develop into chronic constipation, parents need to know how to handle the behavior and when to consult a pediatrician. See What You Need to Know about Constipation, page 58, for more information.

Daytime Bladder Control

Your child must go through the same three learning steps when it comes to urination. But think of how much more subtle the body's cues are when it comes

to urinating. That explains why lots of twenty-four-month-olds are aces at knowing they've wet their pants or are in the process of urinating, but don't quite "get" how to tell that they are *about* to urinate.

Some parents have found that their child is better able to make the connection between feeling full of urine, urinating, and feeling wet when she's allowed to run around bare at home.

Nighttime Bladder Control

It makes sense that nighttime bladder control comes last. A sleeping child has to be pretty thoroughly attuned to her body to get the "bladder is full, gotta go" message in the middle of the night. If your child is a heavy sleeper, it may take several years before she's dry all night. Most experts advise that you don't sweat it if your child still occasionally wets his bed at age five or six. Talk to your pediatrician if the behavior persists or if you're worried about it (see Dry at Night, page 54).

Other Signs of Readiness

While your child is learning bladder and bowel control, he may be sending you other signals that he's ready to potty train. A ready child is learning to pull his pants up and down. In fact, he will start to show an interest in dressing himself. He may even be moving into a whole new "do it myself" phase of independence.

Before training can begin, your child needs to be able to make his way from room to room to get to the potty, and he must understand what the potty is and what you expect him to do with it. He should be able to follow basic directions, such as "throw the ball," "get the book," or "sit on the potty."

Some children suddenly become downright fastidious and begin to hate the feeling of being dirty or being in a messy room. I've known toddlers who have a royal fit when they get food between their fingers or who cry loudly during finger painting. These children's interest in cleanliness and order is a sign that they're maturing. They may be ready to understand that just as there's the right spot to put away their picture books, there's an appropriate place to put feces and urine, too.

A potty-ready child may also show an interest in being a "big kid" by copying Mom and Dad more, comparing herself to "babies," and rejecting her diapers. A child who finds imitation fun and entertaining may enjoy being introduced to how Mommy and Daddy use the toilet.

Parents need to understand and watch for these gradual developments before starting actual potty training. The most important thing for parents to remember is that there is no real "right" age or time for it. It's all internal, and has to come from your child. Think of how great he'll feel when he lets you know that he's ready and then has a smooth transition out of diapers. Think of how crummy he'll feel if he has lots of accidents or is forced to try something he thinks is scary or too difficult. I've seen parents pat themselves on the back for their great toilet training techniques, but the person who really deserves the pat is the child.

Once you have a handle on how your child learns and develops, it's easy to reject those "train your child all in one day" approaches to potty training. They rarely work unless a child has shown all the signs of readiness and has plenty of body awareness and control. If that's the case, there's no need to arbitrarily train in one day; your child will be trained very quickly all on her own timetable.

Differences Between Girls and Boys

Common wisdom holds that boys take longer than girls to potty train. However, this isn't entirely accurate. It may not take longer for a boy to be trained if you wait until the boy is ready. In other words, a boy may be ready a little later than a girl is. If you wait until he's ready, he may learn just as quickly as a girl does.

It's more accurate to say that, on average, boys become trained later than girls. But we're only talking about a matter of months here, not years. Why the lag? Theories abound.

ANATOMY OF
a Child Who Is Ready to Potty Train

You need to put yourself in your child's shoes for a while to understand all that's involved in learning to use a potty. Here are some of the more obvious physical, emotional, and mental developments your child will need to experience before a potty training regime can be effective. For more on readiness, see Checklist: Is My Child *Really* Ready? on page 33.

- Understands body's cues such as a feeling of fullness, pressure
- Can follow directions
- Is in a good mood; has expressed interest in the potty or in wearing underpants
- Knows what a potty is
- Knows when she's wet
- Can pull pants up and down
- Interest in cleanliness

Theory 1: The boys have different equipment

Girls urinate and defecate sitting down. For them, it's a one-position process. Boys, of course, can sit while having a BM and stand while urinating. Having more than one choice naturally complicates the process.

Theory 2: The potty trainer is usually female

Whether your boy is learning potty skills at home or preschool (or both), his trainer(s) will most often be female. From a basic instruction point of view, this shouldn't make a difference. But when it comes to role modeling, it may be harder for a boy to relate to mom's demonstrations since his equipment doesn't match hers. Another factor: Mom may not feel so comfortable demonstrating when her child is of the opposite sex.

Theory 3: The boys are too busy playing to worry about training

Very active boys are likely to forget about anything but what they're involved in at the moment. Going to the bathroom isn't high on their to-do lists. This theory holds that because he's preoccupied with whatever he's doing, a boy may be less tuned in to what his body is telling him. He's not paying attention to any of those "I gotta go" cues.

Theory 4: Boys are more concerned that part of their bodies (i.e. the penis) might fall off and be flushed away

Sometimes boys and girls are afraid of the loud flushing noise the toilet makes. And child development experts point out that both sexes may worry that they're flushing part of themselves away when they see their bowel movement disappear. Although some parents have noticed this phenomenon in their boys, I've never seen or heard any research that confirms that boys are more worried about this than girls, but then this isn't a topic with a tremendous base of research!

I have heard a parent inadvertently introduce this idea to her son who seemed upset after a successful visit to the potty. "Oh honey," she said, "why the tears? You put the poo-poo right where it's supposed to go, and it's all gone away. Your penis didn't go bye-bye. It's still here. You're still here. Everything is okay." I could almost see the wheels turning in the poor kid's head: *My penis didn't go bye-bye?! Yikes. Maybe not this time, but it might happen next time?! Forget it, I'm outta here.*

If your son expresses a concern about his penis or testicles being flushed away, be sure to comfort him and guarantee him that this has never happened. Show him that it may look as if his testicles disappear when he's sitting on the potty, but when he stands up, there they are.

Theories aside, a boy who is ready to begin toilet training will show the same signs of readiness as a girl (see Checklist: Is My Child *Really* Ready? page 33). Watch for all the cues, give it a little time after you detect the readiness signals, and then ease into training. Don't forget to have Dad get involved.

The Case Against Rushing

Even though common sense tells us that we shouldn't—and can't—rush a child onto the potty, the outside world sometimes seems to be conspiring against us. Relatives may tsk-tsk about how "late" your child is and tell rosy stories about how *you* were completely trained by the time you were a year old. Your best friend reminds you that her daughter has been trained for months. The neighborhood daycare center or mother's-day-out program may require that children be trained before they enroll. Or your son or daughter may not be able to "graduate" to a bigger kids' class in preschool until he or she is out of diapers.

These external pressures can gnaw away at you until you're convinced that you and your child are the turtles of toilet training. This is a good time to remind yourself that this isn't a race. If you keep your eye on the real prize—a smooth and happy transition from diaper to potty—you'll be better able to focus on your child's needs and timetable instead of somebody else's. It can't be said often enough: Your child has to be the one to decide when training starts.

You'll know he's ready if you watch for the readiness signals. Preparing him for toilet training is one thing; starting training before he's ready is quite another. In fact, jump-starting toilet training may be detrimental to a child's emotional and physical well-being. What are the pitfalls?

You could make your child feel like a failure. If your child isn't ready to use the potty, all the cajoling and teaching and training in the world isn't going to help. She's not ready. And when she senses that she has disappointed you, she'll feel awful. If she feels bad enough, the negative feelings could color her potty training experience when she *is* ready.

Potty training can become so stressful that the child can become sick or develop bad habits. Some experts maintain that overzealous potty training causes some children to withhold their bowel movements. It's unclear whether they're reluctant to have a BM because the training is so intense or whether they feel their parents are trying to take all their control away from them, and the BM is something that they can stay in charge of.

Not all children who hold in their BMs are doing so because they were trained too soon or pushed too hard. It may be that a child is afraid that she's losing part of herself when she has a BM. In any case, holding in bowel movements can turn into chronic constipation (see What You Need to Know about Constipation, page 58).

Potty training can turn into a terrible power struggle. You really can't make a toddler do something he doesn't want to do. Some parents get very peeved that their child just won't do this little thing—going in the potty—for them.

Toilet training your child is not about doing something for *you*, the parent. It's about your child learning to do something for herself. You can't control her bladder and bowels—she has to.

Not to mention that you'll literally hurry up to wait. There's a long-standing theory that says if you start training at twenty months, you finish at thirty

HOW TO
Dos and Don'ts for a Gentle Start

Although you shouldn't expect your child to have bladder or bowel control when he or she is under two, there are ways to set the stage for successful potty training while your child is still in diapers.

DO

- Respond as soon as possible when your baby or child has a wet or dirty diaper. This may help him begin to understand the difference between wet and dry.
- Chat while you're changing his diaper. "We're taking off that wet diaper and putting on this nice dry one." Sounds basic, but it further reinforces the wet/dry concept.
- Comment positively if your child has a dry diaper.
- Give names to body parts and elimination. Do this only in casual conversation. If your child pees on the floor while getting into the tub you can say, "Look, urine is coming out of your penis. You're making pee-pee."
- Praise him when he (accidentally) manages to urinate in the potty before a bath.
- Give up a little privacy for your child's sake. There's nothing like a live role model to get a child thinking about a new skill. If you feel comfortable, let your child watch you in the bathroom and tell him what you're doing. There's plenty of time later to teach the importance of privacy.
- When you notice that your child is straining to have a bowel movement, point out to him: "You're pushing poo-poo out of your bottom into your diaper. Someday you'll push that into the potty instead, like Mommy and Daddy do."

DON'T

- Make disparaging remarks about the contents of any diaper, even when it deserves the "stinker of the year" award.
- Send the message that going to the bathroom is an embarrassing or disgusting activity.
- Scold or discourage your child's curiosity about his body or bodily functions.
- Rush your child to do things beyond his level.
- Expect anything like overnight success.

months; if you start at twenty-eight months, you finish at thirty months. I'm not saying that thirty months old is the magic age for success on the potty. The point is that there is a wide window of opportunity for potty training. If you wait until your child is ready, it won't take nearly as long for him to catch on. And the training will be much more pleasant.

That's not to say that there aren't so-called "experts" out there who'll say that an early start is smart. I've even heard it suggested that you begin training your child when he is more malleable and agreeable, before the terrible twos and signs of toddler independence set in. You can certainly prep your child for potty training in some nondamaging ways. You can applaud a dry diaper, for instance. But without essential bladder and bowel control—which most children don't develop until they're twenty months old or older—real training can't begin. And while your child may appreciate all that applauding at eighteen months old, she'll appreciate it just as much (maybe more) a year later, when she's more aware of just what it is that she's done that's worthy of such praise.

CHAPTER TWO

Get Set

Remember *PPPPP*: Prior Planning Prevents Poor Performance! Planning for potty training involves preparing you, the parent, as much as your child. You need to be armed with knowledge and the right equipment before you can embark on a potty training plan.

This chapter helps you prepare by answering the following common questions about toilet training:

- What words should we use to identify urine and feces?
- What kind of potty should we buy?
- How should we dress our child for potty training success?
- What is the difference between pull-on disposables and underpants?
- How and when do we discuss potty training with our child's caregiver?

Do You "Wee" or Do You "Pee"?

Did you ever imagine that you'd have to spend even a moment of your adult life thinking about what you're going to call a bowel movement? Or debating the effectiveness of the expression "tinkle" versus "pee-pee?" Chalk it up as just another of the many unexpected joys of parenthood.

I was once talking with some parents when they moved into a discussion about "wee-wee" and "pee-pee," which became rather heated. One mother insisted that pee-pee was what came out of the wee-wee while another parent said that wee-wee was the same thing as pee-pee. Sounds like a ridiculous discussion of potty semantics, but in the case of toilet training, what you call the different parts of your child's body and what comes out of them matters indeed.

In order for a child to be comfortable talking about his body and how it works, parents must first be comfortable, too. That means deciding *before* you start training on terminology that won't make you giggle or blush or cringe. You and your partner both need to be OK with the language, and it needs to feel natural (not too formal or too dorky) to your child. Instead of urine and feces, for instance, you may first want to use "wee-wee" and "doo-doo," or "pee" and "BM."

During my preteen years as a baby-sitter, I worked for one family whose bathroom vocabulary surprised me. I vividly remember the harried mom rushing out the door hollering, "Remember to remind Johnny to urinate." I did not come from a family where "urinate" was used in everyday conversation, and so I thought her comment was hilarious. But four-year-old Johnny knew and understood the word and didn't think twice about saying it or doing it when and where he was supposed to. He was completely comfortable with the terminology his parents used. I was the one with the problem. It's a good thing I didn't have to ask him whether he needed to defecate; I would have died laughing.

Now that I'm a parent, I can say the word *defecate* without going into hysterics. That's not to say I chose to use "urinate" and "defecate" when potty training my daughters. Most parents don't. I also rejected the expression "grunt," which a Southern friend told me her grandmother taught her for having a bowel movement. My husband and I were just fine with "pee-pee" and "poo-poo." We graduated to "bowel movement" and the euphemistic "Do you have to use the bathroom?" as the kids have gotten older, but that's about it. It's unlikely that "defecate," "urinate," or "grunt" would ever spring to our lips naturally. And that's the key: Be natural. Ca-ca, poop, wee-wee, doo-doo, tinkle, whatever—as long as the words are fairly accurate and easy to understand, and aren't offensive to the general public (because rest assured your child will announce them to the world), they should work just fine.

As for what to call the openings from which all this stuff flows, most experts do suggest that you use labels that are anatomically correct. At our house we used vagina, penis, and the general-purpose "bottom." Since we didn't have nicknames for other parts of our daughters' bodies, it didn't make sense to refer to their vagina as a wee-wee or some such.

Recently our eight-year-old asked us why we never called the hole in her bottom "rectum" (she'd been studying anatomy in school). Did I tell her that I just couldn't imagine ever saying "wipe your rectum"? I did not. I just said "My, aren't you smart. That is the appropriate term for the hole in your bottom. I bet you know how to spell it, too." Her question reminded me, though, that it's wise, as potty training progresses to explain that what you call "pee-pee" is also called urine, that "poop" is called feces, that the hole in your bottom is also called a rectum, and so on. If you work these terms into your regular conversations about your child's body, they'll be accepted without embarrassment.

The Potty Training Fashion Police

In an effort to promote your child's self-esteem and ability to do things on her own, you'll want to dress her appropriately for her potty adventures. See How To: Dress for Potty Training Success on page 20 for clothing choices that enhance, not sabotage, toilet training.

Do clothe your child in outfits that are easy to put on and (most important) easy to get off. As you might imagine, time is really of the essence when you're dealing with a toddler who's learning to use the potty. He definitely doesn't have time to unbuckle, unzip, or unsnap. She can do without the tights or tucked-in shirt. Avoid anything that's long and floppy, which could dangle its way into the toilet.

It's also wise to always have several spare sets of clothing on hand—in your bag or in your child's backpack, in the car, in his cubby at preschool. Tuck in a few plastic bags for storing wet clothes away from dry ones.

HOW TO
Dress for Potty Training Success

Thumbs Up

Elastic waistbands: These are a cinch for little kids to pull down and up.

Velcro closings: The next best thing to elastic waistbands. Velcro is much easier to deal with than a snap, button, or zipper.

Crop shirts: If the weather permits, go for a shirt that's cut short or hangs loose instead of one that's long or tucks in. A short shirt gives your child easier access to his pants. Some parents even pin up or shorten their child's tops during potty training.

Skirts: The advantage of a skirt over a dress is that your toddler can be taught to pull down the skirt and panties at the same time (just like pants or shorts).

Going bare: Encourage a stop at the potty whenever your child is bare—before a bath, at the pool, and so on.

Thumbs Down

Overalls: If your child does manage to get the shoulders undone in time, the straps will invariably hang into the toilet.

Zippers, snaps, or buttons: Even if your child is a whiz at undoing these on a doll, don't expect her to be able to undo these on her own clothes.

Belts: Most kids don't have the dexterity to unbuckle a belt, especially when they're in a hurry.

Dresses: A dress can be very confusing in the heat of a potty moment because you have to pull up the dress, then pull down the panties. Whoops, too late.

Tights: This just adds another layer to worry about getting pulled down in time—and to dribble on.

Jumpsuits and snowsuits: Any garment that's one piece is bound to be difficult to get off—and back on.

The Right Equipment

It's time to arm yourself with information about the three Ps: potties, pull-on disposables, and panties. You'll want to take a look at what's available while you're still relaxed—before the training begins. You can stock up on these items later, when you get to the three steps of training (see A Three-Step Potty Plan, page 32), but do your research now.

A Child's Potty

There are about a zillion children's commodes on the market these days in a variety of colors, shapes, and styles (see Buyers' Guide: Potty Pros and Cons, page 24, and Checklist: Choosing a Child's Potty, page 22). Some parents take their child along on the potty shopping trip and let him pick out a model he likes. As long as it's comfortable, convenient, and safe, your child's choice will probably be as good as the next one. Better, maybe, because he'll feel more invested in training since he picked out his own commode.

Many parents decide to buy more than one potty, in part because they can't quite decide where to put their child's commode. If your home has two main bathrooms on two floors, you may wish to have a potty in the bathroom that your child uses near her bedroom and another potty in a downstairs bathroom near the kitchen or family room.

It's also a good idea to have a portable potty that you can take with you. When we lived in San Francisco, we had a child's potty that went everywhere with us in our van. There just weren't enough conveniently located public rest rooms, or unisex bathrooms for my husband to use with the children, for us to feel comfortable without it.

If we went for a long walk on the beach or to a very crowded museum, our daughters knew that they could use the car potty before or after these outings. They weren't at all shy about using it (in the privacy of the van, of course) and we made sure to keep a big supply of double-duty trash bags in which to dump the contents. (There's nothing worse than returning to a car that's been sitting in the hot sun for hours and realizing you forgot to empty the potty—although such an oversight will only happen once.)

We kept what we called the "go-go potty" in the van for emergencies long after both girls were trained, until one day I opened the back of the van too quickly and out the potty rolled down one of San Francisco's famous hills. I thought it was fairly humorous (and I did go retrieve and toss it), but the kids were genuinely upset. That potty had helped them earn a little bit of independence, and even though they didn't need it anymore, they were sad to see it, quite literally, go.

If your child is leery of public bathrooms because the toilets are so huge, consider purchasing a seat adapter to tuck into your purse or bag. Models are available that fold up into a small, easy-to-tote package.

CHECKLIST
Choosing a Child's Potty

It seems as if pint-size potties come in almost as many colors, sizes, and styles as diapers do. To help you narrow down your choices, keep the following questions in mind when potty shopping.

Safety and Comfort

✔ Can my child fall off the potty?

✔ Will she be able to rock it or wiggle it and tip it over? Is it stable?

✔ Are there any sharp or pointed pieces? Is it made of smooth, molded plastic?

✔ Does it pass a pinch test? Are there any movable parts or pieces that slide that might pinch a chubby little thigh or bottom?

✔ Does it have handles?

✔ Is the seat the correct size for my child's bottom?

✔ Is there a small backrest or back piece?

✔ If there is a safety shield, is it removable?

Convenience

✔ Do you want to pick up the entire commode to pour the urine into the toilet or slide out a removable cup?

✔ Does the potty need to be small enough to be portable or packable? Does it need to fit into the trunk or backseat of your car?

✔ Are you looking for a potty that will do double duty (both stand on the floor and fit onto your standard commode)?

✔ Does it have a shield to discourage spraying and to encourage boys to direct the penis toward the bowl?

Aesthetics

✔ Should the potty have a lid?

✔ Do you care whether it's white or fire-engine red?

✔ Does it matter that it resembles a zoo animal instead of a traditional toilet?

Pull-On Disposables versus Cloth Training Pants

At some point in your child's potty training preparation, you'll think it's the right time to move from diapers to panties. Many parents carry this out in stages and try a period of pull-on disposables or cloth training pants first. Both are good choices because they let your child practice pulling her pants up and down and are an acknowledgement that she's on the road to under-pants. Training pants are usually cotton underpants with a very thick layer of absorbent cotton all around. They won't keep your child's clothes dry; dispos-able pull-ons made of diaper material will.

Which is better? That's a decision you'll have to make based on what you know about your child and what stage of training he's in. You can treat pull-ons as a tiny step up from diapers and introduce them at the same time as you bring out the potty. This is for the child who's shown some signs of readi-ness. Right before you start training, buy a box of pull-ons. They usually come in sizes based on a child's weight. If training goes well, you'll probably need slightly fewer of these per day than diapers. Cloth training pants are more appropriate for a child who's already had some success going on the potty. They can be an interim step between pull-ons and real underpants. Cloth training pants are usually sized by age.

The Joy of Underpants

For many children—boys or girls—being able to wear underpants is the ultimate pleasure. Some girls like ruffly ones; some prefer panties that sport their favorite fairytale heroine. Boys, too, like to wear their sports and cartoon heroes on their underpants; others go for plain underpants like Dad's. The key is to not intro-duce underpants too early or your child will feel terribly disappointed that he sprayed Mickey or that she drenched Minnie. Underpants are best saved for when child and parent are feeling quite confident of success. If you introduce them too soon, their incentive value will be lost.

The Childcare Factor

If your child spends all or part of his days with a caregiver other than your-self, it's important to make sure your toilet training styles and philosophies mesh *before* training begins. How a caregiver handles the transition from dia-pers to the potty can make or break your own efforts.

BUYERS' GUIDE
Potty Pros and Cons

There are four basic potty choices:

ONE-PIECE CHAMBER POT

This starter model sits comfortably low to the ground. It's becoming obsolete, though, and can be hard to find. Mostly available as hand-me-downs. Usually under $10.

POTTY WITH CUP

Slightly larger than the chamber pot, the cup model makes cleanup easier. Older children can empty their own cup. $10 and up.

Convertible potty

Two-in-one models function as a stand-alone potty and as an adapter ring. The top pops off and fits onto a standard toilet seat. $10 and up.

YOUR OWN TOILET WITH AN ADAPTER RING

The least expensive option, adapter rings typically range in price from $5 to $15. The more expensive ones come with a step stool. Some models even fold up and have their own case for travel. This is a good option for the older or larger child who's not afraid to climb up onto the adult toilet.

CHAMBER POT	POTTY WITH CUP	CONVERTIBLE POTTY	ADAPTER RING
Pros			
• Simple; one piece • Low profile makes it easy for toddlers to get on and off • Lightweight and compact • Portable • Inexpensive	• Cup makes cleanup easy • Some models come with lids • Smaller versions are quite portable	• Does double duty: use as a stand-alone on floor or use as an adapter ring • Has convenience of cup • Some come with lids • Some models convert into step stools	• Gets child used to big potty right away • Saves expense of child-size potty • Great for traveling or trips to the mall • Nothing to empty
Cons			
• Have to tip the entire potty into the toilet to clean or empty • Because of its light weight, child may be able to scooch it across the bathroom floor like a riding toy • Too small for larger children • Hard to find	• Child may need to graduate to a larger child's potty before moving to adult-size toilet	• Space hog compared to other models • More difficult to clean because of more parts • Not very portable compared to others	• Logistics of climbing up on big potty too scary for some toddlers • May hinder child's independence: Few children can get up without help or use of stool • Important to get a good non-wobbly fit • Needs to be removed for adult use

Whether your child is in a daycare center or preschool, or with a caregiver or relative part of the day, it's wise to discuss your potty training philosophies with anybody who is changing your child's diaper or helping him get to the bathroom. It will only confuse your child if he's exposed to different approaches to potty training.

It may never occur to you when your child is not yet two years old that you need to have this conversation with a caregiver. But unless you get it all out on the table you won't know your caregiver's thoughts on toilet training. If she's over fifty, she may believe, as many grandparents do, that sooner is better. She may have cultural beliefs that a healthy child should be trained early (in some Latin American countries babies are routinely potty trained by eighteen months, for instance). Your child's preschool may be laying down toilet training groundwork that doesn't match your own theories. For instance, the school may be so large that children who wet themselves stay wet for longer than you'd like. Or the caregiver may think potty accidents are a punishable offense. You won't know unless you ask (see Checklist: Potty Training Questions for Your Childcare Center, page 27).

Finding the Right Daycare Center

Both my daughters were in daycare centers during their toilet training years, so I've had two experiences with outside potty training help; one was positive, the other negative. The good experience was so outstanding it made toilet training seem effortless. The bad experience was so miserable that I eventually moved my child to a different preschool. It took several months for her to unlearn some bad habits.

The big difference between the two methods of potty training? Flexibility. One school went with the flow (so to speak) and adjusted its method to each child. The teachers and management believed in teamwork and regularly consulted with parents. The other school had one way and one way only of potty training, and if your child wasn't ready or didn't respond well to their methods, tough. Here are my two stories, one inspiring, the other a cautionary tale.

A Daycare Success Story

Halley Rose was in a class of six to eight children who were all twenty-four to thirty-six months old. The classroom had its own bathroom with a couple of child-size toilets.

CHECKLIST
Potty Training Questions for Your Childcare Center

✔ Do you have a written policy regarding potty training?

✔ What is the center's philosophy?

✔ How is the subject of toilet training introduced?

✔ When is the subject of toilet training introduced?

✔ Do caregivers keep logs of a child's bowel movements and wet diapers?

✔ Is there a certain age by which the center wants a child to be trained?

✔ What role do parents play in the potty training plan?

✔ What kind of progress reports should parents expect? Daily? Weekly?

✔ Does a child need to be out of diapers before he or she can move to the next class?

✔ Are there child-size bathrooms?

✔ Are the bathrooms near or in the children's room? Are they shared with older kids?

✔ Will boys and girls be using the same bathroom? At the same time?

✔ Do children go together or one at a time?

✔ Do you allow children to wear disposable pull-on training pants?

✔ Do you reward potty successes?

✔ Do you teach boys to urinate sitting down or standing up?

✔ How do you deal with an accident? What do you call it and how is it handled?

✔ What terminology do you use? In other words, do you use *BM* and *urinate*, *pee* and *poo*?

✔ Is peer pressure used to encourage a child?

The teachers began monitoring when the kids urinated or had a bowel movement. If the child was developing a regular pattern of going to the bathroom and seemed interested, and if the parents had suggested that perhaps the child was ready to start thinking about the potty, the teacher would have the child visit the bathroom at appropriate times of the day. Success was praised, but the teachers didn't make a huge deal out of it.

A child who was regularly using the potty, or was indicating to the teacher when he had to go, could come to school wearing pull-on disposable underpants if he wished. The teacher and parents would discuss this in advance.

Again, the transition to pull-on underpants was kept low key, but the kids caught on pretty quickly that this was something to be proud of. Success with pull-on disposables meant the child could wear regular panties. Pull-ons or diapers could still be worn at naptime if the child (or parent) requested.

It was all quite laid-back and very effective. Kids were potty trained practically without knowing it because it just felt natural to them. And one child was never compared to another, so the three-year-old boy who was still wearing disposable underpants was in no way made to feel like a slowpoke. My daughter was trained by twenty-seven months and never looked back. No accidents, no setbacks—not even when she became a big sister at twenty-nine months of age.

A Daycare Disaster

If only things had gone so well with my second daughter, Gracie. At ten months old Gracie went to a very large school with children from three months old to second grade. Very progressive, or so its directors thought. The school allowed only cloth diapers and rubber pants (all provided by the school) and seemed quite eager to move little kids out of diapers.

At age two, children progressed to an older group and were expected to be able to use the bathroom. To prepare the toddlers for that move, here was this school's drill:

- At twenty months, a child stopped wearing diapers, except at naps.
- Parents were asked to send their child to school in underpants. No pull-on disposables. No diapers. No regard for the child's stage of readiness.
- Children were encouraged to go to the bathroom at regular times and to let teachers know when they had to go. Within four months (by two years old), each child was expected to be trained and to be out of diapers completely, even at naps.
- When they wet, children were allowed to go bare or stayed wet for a while.

Here's what happened to my child: At first, the freedom of not wearing a bulky cloth diaper thrilled Gracie. (Who wouldn't be thrilled?) By twenty-two months of age she managed to get to the potty on time (or the teachers managed to get her there on time) for a couple of weeks. Ah, success for one so young!

But not so fast. When Gracie wet her pants and was allowed to stay wet, she wasn't uncomfortable, embarrassed, or upset. After a few times, she just got used to it. The feeling of being wet wasn't a signal to her to change clothes or to try to stay dry next time. So what was the incentive to go to the potty? There wasn't one. Every night when I picked her up she was wet or bare. It was very clear to me that the message she received from that particular training was Why bother? She definitely wasn't responding to their method of training.

A major flaw in this approach was that it had no regard for each child's developmental level or for how parents wanted their child to be trained. Here was a child who may not have been ready to be trained or didn't respond to a rigid training method. As a result, she was sort of half trained and developed some bad habits that were very difficult to break.

After several months of trying to work out philosophical differences with the preschool (who tried to make me feel that I was the problem), I moved Gracie to a new school where wet and bare bottoms were not part of the plan. Gracie caught on to their potty routine almost immediately (probably because at twenty-eight months of age she was ready to train). When she did wet her pants, a teacher immediately helped her find her dry clothes. She changed herself, put her wet stuff in a plastic bag, washed her hands, and went back to playing. This wasn't a punishment, but it wasn't fun either—and it interrupted her play. She soon realized it was easier and faster to just run to the potty when she needed to go.

The moral of both stories: even if your child is in someone else's care most of the day, potty training is *your* business. It's a good idea to learn as much as you can about the potty training ground rules and to change them to fit your child if you have to.

CHAPTER THREE

Go!

You've decided what you're going to call your child's body parts and the process of elimination. You've picked out a child's potty and have a closet full of easy-on and easy-off clothes. You've discussed potty training with your child's daycare center or other caregivers. *You're* all ready to go. But is your child?

How do you ever *really* know when your child is ready to begin potty training? That's certainly the million-dollar question. And there is no easy answer. After all, with children you never really know anything for sure. You probably weren't certain she was ready for the transition from bottle or breast to cup, or from crib to toddler bed, either. The best you can do is pay attention to your child and have a good idea what "ready" looks like. Watch for the readiness cues (see Checklist: Is My Child *Really* Ready? on page 32) and go from there.

When you get the green light, it's time to help your child make the gradual transition from diapers to underpants and the potty. Remember this *is* a transition—a step-by-step process. For most families it's a one-step-forward, two-steps-back sort of deal. You've armed yourself with all the right equipment and lots of knowledge, just make sure you don't forget the most important thing of all: patience.

CHECKLIST
Is My Child *Really* Ready?

For most toddlers, the first signs of readiness appear between twenty and thirty months of age. Your child should display most of the following signs before you start training.

✔ Pulls own pants up and down

✔ Shows an interest in dressing himself

✔ Seems gung-ho to "do it herself"

✔ Knows what a potty is and what it's for

✔ Is able to navigate from room to room to get to potty

✔ Sits on the potty by himself

✔ Follows sequential directions, such as "Get the ball, throw the ball"

✔ Shows interest in cleanliness or orderliness

✔ Likes to imitate Mommy and Daddy

✔ Is in a positive phase, showing independence but not saying no to everything

✔ Understands the difference between wet and dry

✔ Indicates when diaper needs to be changed or tries to remove it herself

✔ Recognizes when he's having a bowel movement

✔ Has a dry diaper for several hours for several days in a row

✔ Expresses interest in potty or underpants

A Three-Step Potty Plan

There's no need to start potty training suddenly. That will only startle, confuse, and possibly turn off your child. Instead, gradually introduce the subject and the skills required in three stages: telling, showing, trying. Telling and showing may merge and overlap, but trying should definitely follow the first two. Your child must know what you expect him to do before he can try it himself.

Step One: Telling

Be straightforward and casual when you talk about using the potty so that your child understands that potty training is a normal, natural step. Your matter-of-factness will also convey that you have confidence in your child's abilities to catch on. Look for teachable moments in which you can discuss potty training in a low-key, interesting way.

Body Talk

You can use your child's curiosity to raise his body awareness. Toddlers are naturally interested in their bodies and like to point to various parts and label them. The child's bottom and vagina or penis naturally become a part of this labeling game.

You can take the game a step farther by discussing what each body part does. The nose is for smelling, ears for hearing, penis for going pee-pee, bottom for sitting, hole in bottom for going poop, and so on. Play this game during diaper changes or while you're bathing your child. Keep it casual and fun.

It's never a good idea to scold your child for asking questions or talking about his body—or anybody else's body for that matter. This is how children learn. They have no sense of embarrassment about body parts or bodily functions until you teach it to them.

If your child asks you "Does Grandpa have a penis?" or "Does the mailman poop?" don't overreact. Answer her questions. If she asks Grandpa or the mailman those questions in your presence, you can smooth over any awkwardness by saying "Megan is learning to use the potty and has been learning about how bodies work." And then answer for the folks if they seem put off or startled (or if you think they're going to respond inappropriately): "Yes sweetie, everybody poops and pees. All men have penises and all women have vaginas."

Potty Talk

There are lots of opportunities to bring up the subjects of using the potty and how the body works during your child's day. For example:

- During a diaper change you can say, "That's a wet diaper. You peed in it. Now I'm putting on a dry diaper. Doesn't that feel good?"

- When you visit a rest stop during a trip or visit the bathroom while at the mall you can say, "Mommy drank such a big glass of water, and now my bladder is telling me I need to urinate. I feel full. Let's go in here so I can pee and empty my bladder into the toilet. Then I'll feel better."
- If your child has a pet, such as a cat or dog, he'll see how an animal urinates and defecates. You can say, "Sadie has to pee and poo just like you do. You go in your diaper, she goes in her litter box. I empty her litter box just like I empty your diaper."
- When your daughter stands up to get out of the bathtub and urinates, you can say, "That's pee-pee coming out of your vagina. Someday you'll sit on the toilet and put that into the potty like Mommy and Daddy do."
- If your son pees on the floor, you can say "Pee-pee is wet, isn't it? When it came out of your penis, it made a puddle on the floor. When you learn to go in the potty, your pants and the floor will stay dry."
- When you're touring a preschool or visiting an elementary school, you can point out the child-size toilets that the children use. "Look at that little potty. It's just the right size for you. The children put their pee and poo in there so that they're dry and clean."

Step Two: Showing

If your child has shown several signs of readiness and you've talked the talk, it's time to move on to the showing stage. Showing is sort of like practicing for the real thing. It's another chance to make sure that your child understands your expectations. You can use books and videos as well as role modeling to show your child what going to the potty is all about. In addition, now's the time to unveil a child's potty and, if you choose, to graduate to the kind of diapers that your child can pull up and down himself (see Pull-On Disposables Versus Cloth Training Pants, page 23).

Introducing the Potty

Giving your child her own potty can be treated as either a big, big deal or a low-key event. You know best what your child would most enjoy—and respond to. Some parents don't want to overwhelm the child with a ceremonial unwrapping of her new potty. They know that for their child that would be intimidating and would put too much emphasis on potty training. The child might become upset and reject the potty and the idea of training. Those children may be happier just discovering a little potty in the bathroom one morning. No big deal. If she asks what it is and what it's for, a parent can say, "Oh, that's your potty. We wanted you to have one all your own that's just like ours. When you're ready you can use it," and leave it at that until the child asks more questions.

Other children love big happenings, big events, and anything that has to do with a present. Parents of those children may want to take them on a shopping trip to buy their own potty or make a party out of the appearance of the new bathroom fixture. If the toddler has been talking with his parents about getting a potty when he's ready, this may be an enjoyable milestone for him. Either way of introducing the potty is fine as long as it feels right for you and your child.

If you do make a big deal out of the new potty, let the dust settle before you make another big hoopla over your child's attempts to use it (unless your child insists on trying it out immediately). Too much of a circus or party atmosphere can make the whole act of potty training seem unnatural and forced. The goal is for using the potty to become a natural everyday thing to do. Too much celebrating may even cause your child to rebel a bit. At this age he's still walking a fine line between wanting to please you and resist you.

The potty has arrived . . . so now what? What happens next will, again, depend upon your child's temperament and his state of readiness. If he's curious and rambunctious and ready to try anything, he may ask to sit on the potty. (Before he sits, make sure that you remove any sort of potty shield that might have come with the child's toilet. These shields are designed to help a boy learn to point his penis down into the potty and to prevent spraying, but more than one little guy has injured himself on the projecting shield.)

Go ahead and let him experiment with the potty. But follow his cues. While very interested children may even want to sit on the seat with their pants off, other toddlers may just want to look. Still others will do anything *but* sit on it: stack blocks on it, store markers in it, use it as part of an obstacle course, and so on. That's all part of getting used to it and it's all fine. They may want to take it into their room with them and play with it there. That's OK, too. The potty is theirs. Saying "This is your potty. You can play with it. When you're ready, you can try putting your pee-pee or poop in it," tells the child your expectations without undue pressure.

If you have a choice between a potty of the child's own and a seat adapter, go with the potty, and use the adapter after he has mastered the potty. Why? If you're using a potty-seat adapter on a big toilet (along with a safe and sturdy stepping stool), it's not as easy for your child to feel a sense of owner-ship. Another disadvantage is that it's not always available for the child to use. If another family member has used the toilet, remind that person to put the adapter back on so that it's available when your child wants to look at it or try to use it.

From Diapers to Pull-On Pants

Like introducing the potty, making the move from diapers to pull-on pants can be a major event or an everyday happening. Many parents choose to make it a nonevent and save the big deal for the move to underpants or train-ing pants. That often proves to be the wisest move.

For now, all you need to do is tell your child that he's going to be wearing pull-on diapers from now on and that he can help pull them on and off him-self. Explain that they're pull-on underpants like Mom and Dad wear but that his are more absorbent. Make clear that this is a step toward wearing real un-derpants and using the potty all on his own.

Your child will enjoy it if you give her the responsibility of pulling down the pants and throwing them away when you're changing her. You'll still have to clean up her bottom, but she can then pull on her own fresh pair of disposable pants. Most kids think this is pretty darn cool.

This is also the time to make sure that your child is wearing potty-friendly clothing (see Potty Training Fashion Police, page 19). He won't be able to get to his pull-on disposable pants if first he can't get his blue jeans down.

Role Modeling

Some parents are squeamish about going to the bathroom in front of their children. That's natural since many of us had lessons about privacy drilled into us for years. But this is one family situation where a lack of privacy is a good thing.

One of the best ways for your child to understand all that's involved in us-ing the toilet—pulling down pants, sitting, going, wiping, flushing, washing hands—is to watch you doing it. If you're comfortable with a little sightseer in the bathroom with you occasionally, then invite him in. If not, don't force the issue. Your child could pick up on your discomfort and associate your awkwardness with potty training or with his body. You certainly don't want to make a negative impression on your child. And when your child is in the bathroom with you, keep it low key. It shouldn't be a hyped up event where "now we're going to watch Mommy pee."

SUCCESS STORIES
The Power of Role Modeling

"My husband and I were never embarrassed about letting Ross come into the bathroom with us. One day when he was three years old and had shown no interest, I heard some activity while I thought he was napping. Ross had awakened, gone to the bathroom, peed in the toilet, and gone back to bed. He got the idea from watching us. We never bought diapers again."

—*Sue Broadbooks, Lakewood, Colorado*

Just because you're OK with role modeling good potty technique doesn't mean the rest of the world will be (or should be). I came home one night to have the baby-sitter tell me that one of my daughters had asked to watch her using the toilet. The baby-sitter, who worked part-time at a childcare center, was pretty savvy about potty training. She told Halley Rose that it was OK for family members to watch each other but that other folks liked to use the bathroom in private. When Halley responded by asking, "You do go pee and poop, don't you?" the baby-sitter was quick to reassure her that everyone did.

If there's an older sibling in the house, your child may have watched the potty-going drill a hundred times already and that's great. An older sister or brother can be a wonderful role model. But it's still helpful for a girl to see her mom using the bathroom if the sibling is a boy, or for a son to see Dad if the sibling is an older sister.

When you're using the toilet, suggest that your child sit on his own little potty. He can do it with his clothes on or off; it's his choice. He can demonstrate that he knows how to pull his own pants down and up. If he doesn't want to, don't push it. If he wants to do it all the time but doesn't produce anything, don't sweat it. The showing phase is really more about learning than about trying. You want your child to have time to get used to the potty and to the new diapers he can pull up and down himself. You want to work explanations of going to the potty into your everyday conversations and life.

Many children also role model potty behavior with stuffed animals or dolls. Just as they pretended to change their plaything's diapers, they'll enjoy sitting Teddy or Babydoll on the pot. When they're playing this game, they're showing you that they understand what the potty is for and that they know what is expected of them. It still may be quite some time before they choose to sit on the little potty themselves, but this type of play is great practice.

Visual Aids

Children's books and videos that teach toilet training help your toddler realize that using a potty is really *his* accomplishment—that potty training is all about him growing up and taking charge. It's not something that parents are arbitrarily inflicting on him.

Such resources are great for all stages of potty teaching—telling, showing, and trying—but they're especially useful during the early stages. You can work in a potty-related book at bedtime and your child won't even know he's "learning" anything. Try "I Can Do It!" on page 68, for a gentle introduction to using the potty.

My oldest daughter was fascinated by the picture in the book *Once Upon a Potty* by Alona Frankel, in which the little girl is bending over and showing the hole in her bottom where the poo-poo comes out. That one illustration got Halley Rose interested in what comes out of where—a stage of body awareness that's necessary before a child can really embrace potty training. (My mother, on the other hand, was shocked when she found her granddaughter looking like a contortionist, trying to twist her body so that she could see her bottom in the mirror.)

Another big hit at our house was a video that featured several very catchy songs. In one vignette, after a little girl successfully uses the potty her entire family breaks into a lusty rendition of "She's a super-duper pooper . . ." I've forgotten the rest of the song, but that one line went through my head for months. And it made a huge impression on my daughter, who thought it was hilarious. She, happily, tuned into the tape's message of pride and self-esteem without ever requesting that we actually sing the songs.

The tape, called *It's Potty Time!*, did a good job of entertaining and teaching (not preaching). It was developed by some smart folks at Duke University and was soft-sell all the way, which is definitely the way to go. If you sit down with a potty book or video and make a big deal of it—"Now Suzie and Mommy are going to learn something. Let's watch carefully . . ."—you're already putting too much emphasis on training.

Step Three: Trying

Now that a child's potty has become a permanent fixture in your home, your child probably has the basics of potty training down, at least in theory. Your next move is to encourage her to try to use the potty. You can do this step-by-step in a gradual, pressure-free way.

You and your child may work through the following eight steps in eight

CHECKLIST
Potty Training Books and Videos for Children

Books

✓ *Dry All Night* by Alison Mack (Little, Brown and Company)

✓ *Everyone Poops* by Taro Gomi (Kane/Miller Book Publishers)

✓ *Going to the Potty* by Fred Rogers (Putnam & Grosset)

✓ *I Want My Potty* by Tony Ross (Kane/Miller Book Publishers)

✓ *Koko Bear's New Potty* by Vicki Lansky (Bantam Books)

✓ *Once Upon a Potty* by Alona Frankel (Barron's)

✓ *P.J. & Puppy* by Cathryn Falwell (Clarion Books)

✓ *Sesame Street's I Have to Go* by Anna Ross (Random House)

✓ *The Potty Chronicles* by Annie Reiner, L.C.S.W (Magination Press)

✓ *The Princess and the Potty* by Wendy Cheyette Lewison (Simon & Shuster)

✓ *The Toddler's Potty Book* by Alida Allison (Price Stern Sloan)

✓ *Toilet Learning* by Alison Mack (Little, Brown and Company)

✓ *Uh Oh! Gotta Go!* By Bob McGrath (Barron's)

✓ *Your New Potty* by Joanna Cole (Mulberry Books)

Videos

✓ *Bear in the Big Blue House: Potty Time With Bear* (Columbia TriStar)

✓ *It's Potty Time* (Learning Through Entertainment/Duke University Medical Center)

✓ *Once Upon A Potty for Her* (Barron's)

✓ *Once Upon a Potty for Him* (Barron's)

✓ *The Big Comfy Couch: Molly's Potty Lesson* (Time-Life Kids)

✓ *Toilet Training Your Child* (Consumer Vision)

✓ *Winston's Potty Chair* (Cinema Visuals Entertainment with the AMA)

months, eight weeks, or eight days. Always remember: you're working on your child's timetable. If she balks at any step of the way, back up to the previous step and take it easy for a while.

1. *Once a day.* Start by suggesting that your child should try to urinate or defecate in the potty one time during the day. Some parents try first thing in the morning; others ask their child to try before bathtime. During this stage, your child is still wearing pull-on disposable diapers. He simply needs to pull them down or be naked when he sits on the potty.

2. *Create the ritual.* By trying at the same time each day, your child will begin to recognize and appreciate the routine. Kids this age love predictable rituals and the same thing/same place/same time of day feeling of using the potty should please them (or at least not alarm them).

3. *Increase potty visits.* Once your child has success on the once-a-day plan (or even if he's not consistently successful but asks to sit on the potty at other times of the day), have him try several times a day. You can gently remind him at those times when he usually needs to go, or at this stage of the game, you can let him decide. He's still in pull-on disposables so accidents aren't a tragedy.

4. *Introduce underpants.* If your child is staying dry for part of the day and using the potty consistently (that is, several visits per day), she may be telling you it's time to make the move to underpants. Have her go to the store and pick them out with you or make a present of a dozen brand-new pairs of panties. Continue to use diapers or pull-on disposables at night.

5. *Encourage regular visits.* After your child has made the transition to underpants, encourage regular, scheduled visits to the bathroom. She may still be learning all of her body's cues that tell her she needs to pee or she may become so engrossed in play that she forgets to go. For a little while, your help in reminding her to go is a good thing.

6. *Expect accidents.* While the switch to underpants may thrill your child, it may also baffle him. He may be shocked when he realizes that they don't work at all like a diaper. When he pees, he immediately feels it running right down his legs.

I remember my daughter having a real "what's going on here?" reaction to her first accident in panties. I told her, "Diapers are like a sponge; they soak up the pee-pee. Underpants don't. When you make pee-pee in your underpants, you'll get all wet. That's why when we wear underpants, we pee and poop into the potty."

Most children genuinely want to keep their brand-new underpants dry and do their best to reach the potty in time. But accidents are to be expected. Help your child get cleaned up and reassure her that she'll be successful next time. Remind her that everyone has accidents and not to worry. You're so proud of her. She's doing great!

7. *Reduce visit reminders.* After a few weeks, let the time between visits and reminders grow, and see how well your child does. You want her to know that she's in charge of her achievement. If you constantly tell her when to go, she'll feel someone else is in control.

It's also beneficial for a child's bladder to fill up and stretch out a little. If it's constantly being emptied, your child will never learn to recognize that really full feeling, and her bladder will take longer to mature and hold more urine.

8. *Give him more freedom.* If all is going well, continue to give your child more and more opportunities to use the bathroom on his own. The more successes he has, the more confident he'll feel. Continue to treat accidents as normal: reassure, help clean up, move on.

When to Back Off

At some point your child may indicate that she's just not ready to try. She may even ask to go back to her pull-on disposable pants or her diapers, which is fine. Your child should never think that returning to diapers is a punishment. Take this as a sign of a child who knows herself, rather than a sign that you or she have somehow failed. You can continue to talk about using the potty in a low-key way and wait until she indicates that she's ready to try again.

How to Praise

Some parents feel like bursting into the Hallelujah Chorus each time their child delivers a little something into the potty. Before you do that, consider what kind of praise your child best responds to. If he's the quiet sort, a gentle pat on the back might suffice.

And consider the purpose of the praise. You want your child to know that you're proud of him and that he's done a good job. You don't want him to think his successes are so important, however, that he's going to start worrying about failure. Nor do you want him to feel a sense of accomplishment because "he made a poop for Mommy." Sorry Mom and Dad, this poop's not for you, it's for your child. He must understand that it's his achievement and that learning to use the potty is for his own good.

When you are praising your child, choose your words carefully. Just as you discipline by pointing out the bad behavior (not calling the *child* bad), you'll want to praise the good *job* and not the child. Be wary, too, of referring

FROM THE TRENCHES
Advice from Moms and Dads
Who've Been Down the Potty Training Path

"Follow your child's lead. When my daughter was almost two, she saw a picture of a little girl sitting on the potty. She asked, 'What's that little girl doing, Mommy?' I said, 'She is going pee-pee on the potty. Would you like to try?' She used the potty and has been doing so ever since."

—*Deborah Hrabinski, Piscataway, New Jersey*

"The best advice I received was to wait until my son was ready, which was at two years and nine months. One day, with no prompting from me, he announced he was potty trained. He had just a few accidents over the next week, and that was that."

—*Sherry Wainz, Toledo, Ohio*

"One day my daughter came to me and said, 'I need to go pee.' 'Okay Marie,' I told her, 'Go on in the bathroom and go!' She did . . . all over the floor! I wasn't explicit enough. After that I kept a jar of M&Ms in the bathroom. When she went in the potty, she was rewarded with an M&M."

—*Deborah Lose-Kelly, Jefferson City, Missouri*

"My advice to other parents is relax, relax, relax. Don't belittle children when they have an accident. Watch for cues that they need to use a rest room. A pet peeve of mine is hearing a parent tell a young child, 'Just hold it.' "

—*Shellie Smith, Williamston, Michigan*

too much to being a "big boy" or a "big girl." Using the potty is one of your child's first baby steps toward independence, and he may not be ready to think of himself as a "big" anything. He shouldn't feel that you're in any way withdrawing attention or affection from him now that he's "big."

The Pros and Cons of Rewards

If your child has shown signs of readiness and if he seems to need a little push to use the potty, some experts say it's just fine to use rewards. A little incentive—a treat, a sticker, or a small toy—might sweeten the deal for a child who's ready and willing to use the potty. The reward may motivate him to practice his new skill and to consistently get to the potty on time.

A reward can't take the place of the child's own desire to learn how to use the potty, however. That's where the experts draw the line. A sticker isn't going to light the fire under a child who isn't the least bit interested in, or ready for, potty training.

If you do decide to use rewards, some parents suggest using a chart or calendar so that the child can map his progress. If the reward is earned only after several successful potty visits, make sure you're not making your child wait too long for the goodie: he'll forget the whole point if the time between the positive action and the reward is longer than a day or two.

To Flush or Not to Flush

That is another question you'll have to answer. There are two schools of thought on flushing during potty training.

The Case Against Flushing

- Many children don't like the noise; it startles or scares them.
- Flushing draws attention to this big swirling hole into which some children fear they might fall and disappear.
- Children can become possessive of their bowel movements and become disturbed by seeing them swept away.

If your child has shown any fear of flushing, don't flush in her presence. To avoid sabotaging your potty training efforts, wait until she's left the bathroom before you flush the big commode or flush away the contents of her

Q&A

"Should I Teach My Son to Urinate Sitting Down or Standing Up?"

Do yourself (and your bathroom walls) a favor: teach your son to pee sitting down. He'll be sitting to make a bowel movement anyway—and urine often accompanies a BM—so sitting will feel normal to him. At first he may just "accidentally" pee into the potty as he's sitting to deliver a BM.

If your son's father models the seated position your child will think it's perfectly OK for boys to sit. Dad can show him how to aim his penis down into the toilet bowl while seated. Another advantage of sitting is that it helps boys focus on the matter at hand instead of on the fun of spraying. More dribbles make it into the toilet. (If your child is in daycare during training, ask whether they teach standing or sitting. You may want your teaching methods to jive.)

When your son has grasped the concept of peeing and pooping in the potty and does it regularly and with some success, he can be taught how to pee standing up. Dad, obviously, should be involved in this training. There are toilet targets and other gimmicks on the market designed to help your son improve his aim. Some parents swear by 'em; others think they encourage fooling around.

If your child vehemently insists on peeing standing up—to the point where he's resisting potty training because he doesn't want to sit—let him stand. There's no value in turning this issue into a power struggle. He may be showing that he really is ready to pee standing up.

little potty. Fear of flushing usually fades in a few months and often disappears by the time your child has graduated to the big toilet.

In Defense of Flushing

- Because it's a fact of life, you may as well have the child get used to the noise, the swirling, the disappearing bowel movements.
- Some kids love to flush and feel it's almost a reward in itself.

If you have a child who loves to flush, you don't have a problem (although be aware that a child sometimes develops an aversion to flushing later).

Those who plan on flushing may want to encourage it even before their child is using the potty. Many children love to flush when they first discover the toilet. They'll flush again and again with absolutely no concern about it. When your child is still in diapers, empty the diaper into the toilet and let her flush the contents away. If your child is nearby and shows an interest, you can invite her to flush the toilet after you've used it. Once she's been going in her own potty for a while, if she has the dexterity she can dump her own urine and feces into the toilet and flush it, too. If she develops any fears of flushing, wait until she's out of the bathroom and flush for her.

Make Potty Time Fun

Make your child's visits to the potty enjoyable and encourage her to actually spend a little time there (but never force her to get on the toilet or to stay on). My daughters loved to sit on their little throne and read a book. My oldest liked to have me squirt a smiley face in lotion onto each of her chubby knees while she sat. She'd play with the lotion and squish it around while we chatted. Then she'd rub the lotion onto her legs and she could say "Goodbye poop" and "Goodbye dry skin" all at the same time. She thought that using the lotion and the potty were both very grown-up things to do and she enjoyed them.

When the Going Gets Rough

What should you do if your child doesn't want to try the potty? If he's very resistant or afraid to use the potty, give it a couple of weeks and try again. He may just not be ready.

If he's just taking a long time to train, remind yourself that this is normal. Make sure you're working on *his* timetable, not anyone else's. Also, take a look at your potty training techniques to ensure that they're a good match with your child. Children are very tuned in to how you're feeling. If you're too intense, your child may be turned off, in part because he's afraid he'll disappoint you by failing.

Why is it that some children don't take to potty training?

Your child may just not "get it." He may be at the point where he knows when he's filling his pants but isn't yet able to anticipate the event. Basically, he's not ready. You can keep talking to him about how it feels right before he has to go, but you may just have to wait until he's a little older.

SUCCESS STORIES
Great Incentives

"We bought a set of fourteen Matchbox cars and Jonathan got to pick one for himself at the end of the day if he managed to stay dry. By the end of two weeks, the cars were gone and he was potty trained."

—Kristi McClellan, San Angelo, Texas

"When we were training our oldest son, Ron, we were in the process of building a cabin. Going to the bathroom meant using an outhouse. I've never seen a better incentive for getting out of the diapers than a trip to that exciting outhouse. He was trained in no time.

"We had built-in plumbing by the time our daughter Greta got to the potty training stage. I had bought a special pretty pair of panties and was saving them for when she was older. She saw them and wanted to wear them *right now*. I said 'Okay, but you can't pee-pee in them. They have to stay dry.' That was all it took."

—Winnie Krueger, Crandon, Wisconsin

"For my two boys, sweets went a long way to motivate them to use the potty. When he was training, our oldest son, Albert, got an M&M each time he used the toilet. Two years later when his younger brother was training, Sam got an M&M if he used the potty and Albert got one, too, for helping Sam. I was worried I would rot Albert's teeth before they were both trained, but it worked so well I didn't want to stop!"

—Sue Murrian, Knoxville, Tennessee

He may be afraid to try to go. Some children are worried about being a failure. Such a child doesn't want to disappoint his parent by not being perfect. Think about your approach to potty training and consider lightening up a little.

She just doesn't want to use the potty—because you want her to! Some children refuse to be controlled and sense (rightly so) that control is what learning to use the potty is all about. It's not simply about them learning to control their own bodily functions, they feel it's about you trying to control them. The more you try to help, the less interested or more resistant she becomes. Try stepping back and giving her the chance to learn her own way. Recognize using the potty for what it really is: part of your child's struggle for autonomy. It shouldn't also become a struggle of wills between you and the child.

He's going though a "no" phase. If "no" and "don't wanna" accompanied by shoving-away motions are your child's main methods of communicating right now, it's safe to say that it's not a good time for potty training. Children go through normal periods of negativism, which is all part of the growing-up and growing-away process. You can keep talking and showing in gentle ways, but it's perfectly OK for your child to stop trying if the timing doesn't seem right.

Too many other things are going on in her world. If your child's life is filled with change right now—new school, new sibling, new home, for instance—she may not be able to focus on learning a new skill. Wait until things have settled down if your child seems stressed or resistant.

A physical problem. Sometimes when children have a hard time training or regress soon after beginning to train, it's because they have a physical problem. You'll want to visit the pediatrician to rule out a urinary infection or constipation.

Teaching the Resistant Child

Sometimes a child is definitely ready but is still totally resistant or aggressively uninterested. You might try:

- **A stepped-up system of rewards.** Choose something the child really likes and consistently provide that reward when he uses the toilet. The reward needs to be very desirable (something more substantial and unique than stickers, for instance) and it needs to be delivered each time. One child I know loved dinosaurs and was allowed to take a little plastic dino out of a container left in the bathroom each time he used the potty. Another boy had a serious fascination with firetrucks. His clever Dad disassembled a huge fire truck and the child was rewarded piece by piece (he got a color picture of the assembled truck with the first piece). When he'd earned all the parts, the Dad and son built the truck together. Once he was in the habit of going, the child never regressed.

This sort of reward or incentive may get the child over the hump of not trying. He may have gotten into the habit of saying no to using the potty and needs you to provide an incentive for him to change his mind.

- **A change of trainers.** If you're the one doing all the potty teaching and it's not working after a long period of trying, consider a changing of the guard. One mother told me her daughter was ready but completely uninterested no matter what the mom did or said. The little girl's aunt came into town for a weekend and "breezed in and had her trained in two days," the mom recounted. The aunt told the child, "Oh, I know you want to use the potty and I know you can do it. We're going to do it this weekend. Let's do it." And the little girl did!

  Why did she decide to use the potty for the aunt and not for the mom? It's hard to know for sure. Maybe she was suddenly just ready. Maybe she saw an opportunity to prove to herself—and to this new person—that she could do it. Maybe Mom had inadvertently pushed too hard and turned her off on toilet training. Maybe her mom hadn't pushed hard enough and the aunt saying "We're going to do it this weekend" was the sort of firm deadline that the child needed.

  The best thing about this story was that the girl felt great and the mom did, too. She wasn't in the least bit peeved that someone else had trained her child because she realized it was her daughter's achievement, not the trainer's. And, frankly, she was just glad to have it done.

- **A change of scenery.** If the weather is warm, move your potty training lessons outside. Bring the child's commode with you and let your child go bare for a while if it feels good to her. She may think it's a fun game to run back to the potty and urinate in it.

  One child I know learned not to wet his pants while on a camping trip, quite by accident. The family had backpacked into a park and were setting up their tent far from any real campground. When the dad set off into the woods to pee behind a tree, the little boy went with him. And how could he resist? Of course he wanted to pee on the tree, too. And he did with great pleasure. In fact, that event became the highlight of the trip for the boy, and he insisted right then and there to be shed of his diaper.

Q&A

"My husband is circumcised but our son is not. What should we tell our son when he notices that he and Dad don't have look-alike penises?"

The answer depends upon the maturity of your son and how much he really wants to know. Parents sometimes overexplain when all the child wants is a one- or two-word answer. The key, of course, is to be matter-of-fact about it. Your husband might say: "Oh, I had a piece of skin taken off my penis when I was a baby, but you still have that skin. So we're a little bit different but mostly we're the same. See, we both can pee-pee in the potty like this . . ."

That may completely satisfy your son. An explanation of the physical difference may be all he needed to reassure him that he and Daddy are both OK. If he asks "Why?" you might try another short answer: "Doctors used to think it was healthier for a baby to have the skin removed but now most think it's okay to leave it on, so Mommy and Daddy decided to leave it." If he continues to be curious, or if he notices that other boy's penises are also different from his, a parent can say "That piece of skin is called the foreskin. Some boys have the skin and some boys don't. It doesn't change how the penis works."

Few children at the age of three or four are going to be able to get a handle on the words "circumcised" or "uncircumcised," but go ahead and use the words if you're comfortable with them. The goal: to reassure your child if he's worried, to answer his question matter-of-factly and quickly. You want to send the message that you're comfortable talking about your child's body and bodily functions so that he'll feel it's OK to ask you anything.

During warm weather, a tree in the backyard can serve as the same kind of incentive. Some parents even paint a target on the tree to make it even more interesting. Once a child gets the hang of not wetting his diaper or himself outside, he's usually ready to carry that behavior back into the house with him.

CHAPTER FOUR

Keep Going

Congratulations! If you've reached this chapter, your child has probably had some success going on the potty. You'll know within a few days if she's really caught on or if she "accidentally" managed to be in the right place doing the right thing at the right time. If that's the case, you shouldn't consider it a major setback. It's usually a signal that your child is not quite ready. Watch for signs of readiness and try again in a few weeks.

Even if your child seems to have caught on, it often takes several weeks or months before using the potty feels truly routine. There will be plenty of dribbles and accidents, and it may be several more months before your child can stay dry all night. There are also lots of new challenges for the newly potty trained child, such as using a public rest room.

Setbacks and New Challenges

There are several reasons a child who has been happily and regularly using the potty suddenly loses interest or turns against the whole process. Here are a few of the more common explanations for why potty training may come to a screeching (or dribbling) halt:

- an illness
- a move
- a vacation
- a new sibling
- a new caretaker
- a parent being away from home

Be especially considerate of and reassuring to your child during these times of stress and know that she'll get back on track when she's gained her equilibrium. If training was well established, gently discourage her from a return to diapers, unless she absolutely insists. If she does, that's OK. Give her opportunities to tell you why she wants to stop using the potty. It's fine to ask gentle leading questions, but don't probe too much or she'll sense that she's disappointing you, or she may rebel and decide that using the potty means too much to *you*.

When you're experiencing a setback, it's important to avoid using judgmental phrases, such as "But you were becoming such a big girl" or "We were so proud of you when you went on the potty, you don't want to disappoint us, do you?" Your pride in the child is important, but the emphasis should be on the child's pride in himself. Remember: He's learning to use the potty for himself, not for Mommy. And you shouldn't use the removal of pride or affection as a threat against the child.

Visiting a Public Bathroom

Your child may also balk at using the toilet when it's in a public place. She may have become accustomed to her potty at home or the small commodes at her preschool but finds the big lavatories with stall after stall intimidating. You have a couple of choices regarding how you handle a public restroom:

- If your child is still in the learning stages and wearing diapers or pull-on disposables, make sure she knows it's all right if she doesn't make it to the bathroom when you're away from home. She should just go right in her diaper and you'll visit the restroom to change her. Let her know your expectations.

- If your child has been just recently trained, tell her that you'll be away from home several hours and that for trips like this, everyone will be more comfortable if she wears pull-on disposables. She'll still have the ability to pull them down and use the public rest room if you get to one on time. But you won't be a nervous wreck (and neither will she) about having an accident or finding a five-person line in the bathroom.

- For the child who's been trained for quite some time but still has accidents occasionally, there's no need to make her relinquish her panties unless she's terribly afraid of public bathrooms or is traumatized by accidents.

Whether your child is wearing diapers, pull-ons, or underpants, tell her in advance that while you're out you're going to visit a public bathroom where lots of people go. The potties may be larger there, there may be lots of them, and she may have to wait in line until she can go. But you'll be there with her to help her.

Make sure you know exactly where the nearest potty is on your outing and, if possible, visit it as soon as you get to your destination. Carry a spare set of underpants, some tissue, and a supply of wet wipes. Some parents also like to take along a portable adapter ring that folds up neatly into a purse. With the familiar ring, the child won't worry about falling into a strange, large toilet.

Your best bet is to use the stall that's designed for people with disabilities. It's larger and you and your child can both fit comfortably into the stall. Be aware though: the toilet in these stalls is usually even taller than regular adult commodes in order to accommodate wheelchair-bound visitors.

The question always arises when it comes to mothers taking boys into the women's rest room and fathers taking girls into the men's room. Obviously a mom taking in a boy isn't nearly as problematic as a dad taking in a girl. It's generally more accepted and there's no chance that the boy will see anybody using the toilet other than his Mom. A girl with her daddy, however, usually has to walk past a row of men urinating into urinals—an embarrassing situation for the men, the girl, and the father. So what's the solution? If your daughter is going to be out and about with Dad, do some careful reconnaissance to find those potties that are unisex. These bathrooms have become more and more popular, possibly because of this very problem. The bathrooms usually have only one stall and sink per bathroom so that a father and his young daughter can go in without embarrassment.

Q&A

"My son deliberately has an accident just to get my attention. How should I handle this?"

You first must be absolutely sure that your child is doing something purposeful, which can be very difficult to determine. If your child has just recently been introduced to the potty, chalk it up as an unintentional accident and leave it at that. If your child has been successfully going to the toilet for several months, look for other clues that he may be trying to get your attention.

One of my almost four-year-old nephews purposely goes into his room and urinates on his rug. This happens on days when he feels that his younger brother is getting all the attention or that he hasn't gotten his way. In effect, peeing on his rug is payback for the all the grievances he has against his family that day. He's probably not able to articulate exactly how he's feeling, but his "accident" helps him release some anxiety and also serves as a cry for attention. It's a combined "Take that" and "Look at me!" signal.

Any time a child calls to us for attention, we want to give it—and we should. But in this case, it's important to separate the attention from the potty accident. The accident should not be earning the attention. First deal with the accident, then deliver the attention.

As most parents realize early on, being annoyed with their child provides a certain kind of attention, even though it's negative. Rather than yelling at the child, it's more effective to say, "I really like being with you and playing with you and will find time to do that every day, but I don't like it when you try to get my attention by wetting your pants."

Calmly and with very little emotion make the child aware that it's his responsibility to help clean up the mess. This shouldn't be a punishment, just a matter-of-fact action. You shouldn't appear to be mad. You could say, "Next time try to get to the potty in time, Andrew. Now let's clean up that mess. You take off your wet clothes, put them in the hamper, and put on clean, dry clothes. Then you can help me clean the rug."

After the cleanup is finished, try to find some special time to spend with your child. This time should not be spent talking about potty training but in doing activities that the child really enjoys.

Dry at Night

Staying dry all night arrives at different times for every child. But it most often happens after your child has daytime control.

Some children stay dry at night shortly after they've mastered daytime dryness, but most kids take several months or even a year or more before they can graduate out of nighttime diapers or disposable pants. In fact, it's not unusual for four- and five-year-olds to wet their beds now and then. Heavy sleepers or slow trainers may take even longer.

There's no need to push nighttime training, even if your child was an instant potty training success during the day. Give her time to relish that accomplishment before rushing headlong toward the next challenge. And before putting your child in underpants at night, watch for signs of readiness (see Checklist: Signs of Dry-at-Night Readiness, page 56), such as few daytime accidents and dry diapers in the morning.

If your child exhibits several signs of readiness and the rest of her life is very low-key and stable, go for the underpants. But be prepared: Cover her mattress with a plastic cover. Make sure you have several pairs of pajamas and sets of clean bed linens for your child. When the inevitable accidents occur, at least your mattress will survive and you'll have plenty of clean, dry clothes and sheets handy.

You might also consider using a waterproof mattress pad on top of your child's bottom sheet. Some parents swear by these pads, which absorb lots of wetness and reduce the number of bed-changings necessary.

Once her bed is set up, there are other ways to pave the road to nighttime dryness:

Control Beverage Intake
Limit after-dinner liquids to the quick rinse and spit after tooth brushing (no swallowing!).

Before-Bed Potty Stop
Make a potty visit the very last thing before bed, after tooth brushing, story time, prayers, everything. If you make the potty stop with no results, and your child is still chattering or awake ten minutes later, try again.

Bedside Potty
A strategically placed potty can help a child remember to go right before bed and first thing in the morning. And, if he—miracle of miracles—does wake in the middle of the night and has to urinate, the potty will be very handy. Put a night-light nearby so that he can see where he's urinating, or paint the potty with glow-in-the-dark paint.

CHECKLIST
Signs of Dry-at-Night Readiness

✔ Has very few daytime accidents

✔ Stays dry during naps

✔ Is mad at self if she doesn't make it to the potty

✔ Keeps dry several consecutive nights

✔ Wakes up in the night or early in the morning to try to get to the potty

✔ Requests underpants at night

First-Thing-in-the-Morning Potty Stop

Quite a few children stay dry *almost* all night and then lose bladder control in the morning, just as they're waking up. Sometimes a rush to the potty right after waking can prevent an early-morning accident. If you typically have to wake up your child in the morning to get him going, you might have some luck hustling him directly into the bathroom or to the potty strategically placed near his bed.

Keep Your Child Warm

Some experts believe that children feel more pressure to "go" when they're cold. Whether this is caused because a "cold" bladder can't hold as much urine or it's just a feeling of fullness is unknown. But if you've ever felt the urge to go to the bathroom the minute you start shivering in the cold, you can probably relate to this. Throw an extra blanket on your child's bed just in case.

Applaud Success

Dry beds earn your child a nice pat on the back. A "Hey, good job, you stayed dry all night" is appropriate acknowledgement of your child's success.

Downplay Accidents

Don't make a fuss over a wet bed. If it happens in the middle of the night and your child asks for help, change and comfort her briefly, have her try to go on the potty (although she probably won't have to), and put her back to bed. If she's wet in the morning when she gets up, get her cleaned up and go on with the morning.

Reassure Your Child

If your child is wetting her bed every night, suggest that she go back to pull-on disposables or diapers for a while. Make sure she knows that you're confident she'll be dry all night before long and that this isn't a sign of failure. You all might be more comfortable waiting a little while before moving to underpants for good.

Parents often wonder at what age they should begin to really worry about their child's lack of nighttime control. Lots of children wet while they sleep. Some have immature bladders, some sleep deeply, some have never paid much attention to their body's "gotta go" signals. Some wet only occasionally; others every night. Many children routinely wet the bed until they're six or seven years old.

If you deal with this calmly and in a reassuring way, your child's self-esteem won't plummet and she won't begin to develop a bad self-image. Wetting while asleep is not necessarily abnormal or harmful to the child, until she starts to feel bad about it. If you or the child's siblings or friends tease or humiliate her about wetting while she sleeps, that's a problem. If she's unable to participate in fun events, such as sleepovers or camping, because of her embarrassment over wetting at night, that's a problem. If you feel as if you just can't stand to change the sheets one more time, that's a problem, too.

In these cases, discuss your child's wetting with her pediatrician. He may want to run tests to make sure she doesn't have a urinary infection or some other physical problem. The doctor may tell you that wetting is nothing to worry about until your child is older, as long as you can handle it without putting more pressure on the child. If the pediatrician thinks your child's wetting warrants it, she may tell you about drugs, nighttime alarms, or other aids to staying dry all night. There is also an excellent book available called *Dry All Night* by Alison Mack (Little, Brown and Company), which has helped parents and children view bed-wetting and its "cure" in a whole new way. You may want to read it first.

DEFINITION
Enuresis

According to *Webster's Dictionary*, *enuresis* is "an involuntary discharge of urine." Wetting while asleep, then, could be called "nocturnal enuresis." This involuntary discharge has also been labeled bed-wetting and sleepwetting. Coined by Alison Mack, author of the picture book *Dry All Night*, sleepwetting is the most politically correct term, since it leaves the bed out of it. After all, she points out wisely, who really cares about the bed? The focus should be on the child.

Q&A

"My daughter still can't stay dry all night and she's almost four years old! Should I talk to an expert about her bed-wetting problem?"

A three- or four- or five-year-old who is wetting the bed doesn't have a bed-wetting problem (called enuresis). The great majority of children are not dry at night until they're four years old—or older. Many kindergarteners routinely wet their beds.

A four-year-old typically sleeps deeply and has a small bladder; she may still be struggling with daytime bladder control. This isn't unusual and doesn't warrant calling a professional. Children achieve night dryness on their own timetable, just as they did daytime dryness.

Problems occur when parents begin to obsess over nighttime dryness and their anxiety passes on to their child. Or a preschool friend teases about kids who still wear diapers at night. If your daughter begins to feel guilty or embarrassed about being wet at night, she may develop poor self-esteem. Feeling bad about herself won't help her become dry at night any faster.

Let her develop night dryness at her own pace. Reassure your child that she will eventually be dry all night and that you'll help her in any way you can. Your suggestions or involvement should be requested by her and your help should be very gentle. Your child may want a potty left by her bed. Or you may suggest that she wait a little longer between bathroom visits during the daytime. This may increase bladder capacity and control. Don't bother to carry your child to the potty in the middle of the night. Not only is this a pain for parents and demeaning to kids, but most experts don't think it speeds up the night-time training process a bit.

If at age six or seven your child is still consistently wetting the bed, talk to your pediatrician about a urine test. A urinalysis will help rule out any sort of kidney or bladder infection. If you feel you can't relax about this issue and that you're unable to stop putting pressure on your child, see a counselor.

What You Need to Know about Constipation

Parents often worry that their child is not having regular bowel movements. In fact, you may still be figuring out what's "regular" for your child. Some children only have one or two bowel movements a week and that's normal for them. Some go every day like clockwork. A toddler who typically has a BM every other day may occasionally deviate from this routine for no significant reason or have a harder BM one day than another. These slight deviations are usually no reason for concern.

If your child seems to rarely have a bowel movement or has hard painful BMs, you should take note. Some children, because they're feeling pressure to potty train or because they're afraid to let go of their BM (which they view as an important part of themselves), begin to hold it in. There is a difference between holding in BMs and having them infrequently. The child who holds it in may be setting off a vicious cycle of constipation. You may actually be able to see or feel the hard BMs collecting in the child's large intestine. It will look like a hard lump protruding from his stomach.

The intestine is flexible and can accommodate this for a while (and in most cases it will shrink back down after the bowels are cleared). The problem is that the harder the BMs get, the more they hurt as they pass through the rectum. Once a child has a hard, painful BM, she's not likely to forget it. Her rectum may become sore or, on rare occasions, even have a small tear. This may cause her to withhold even more BMs. Eventually the anal sphincter will reflexively clamp down to prevent the painful BM from being passed.

Sometimes withheld bowel movements build up and soft stools leak out around the blockage. Parents may mistake this condition for diarrhea, but it is really the result of constipation (see Definition: Encropesis, page 60).

If you suspect your child is holding in hard BMs, talk to his pediatrician. Many doctors will recommend that you stop training for the time being. The idea is to help the child relax and feel it's safe to have a BM. If this means going back to diapers, do it. You want your child to understand that now may not be the right time for going on the potty, especially if all that trying has made him have BMs that hurt. It's OK for him to go back to diapers and have his bowel movements wherever and whenever he wants.

It's important that your child not feel that the return to diapers is a punishment or that he is a failure. Reassure him that he will eventually go on the potty and it won't hurt. Diapers and a postponement of training should feel like a good solution to him. It will give him time to heal and to relax.

Some doctors prescribe a stool softener or laxative, or a high-fiber diet to help the bowels along. And if your child has a tear in her anus, petroleum jelly may soothe it.

The doctor may have a general consultation with you about your potty

DEFINITION
Encopresis

This term is used to refer to the pattern of soiling or fecal leakage that can occur when a child withholds bowel movements. What might look like watery diarrhea to a parent is really soft stools that are leaking out around a rock-hard BM inside the child's large intestine.

If you notice this sort of soiling occurring during potty training or a few weeks after your child has "caught on" to using the toilet, talk to the doctor right away. If he rules out diarrhea or an intestinal upset, you may want to put the brakes on potty training for a while. Encopresis and withholding bowel movements are usually signs that a child is unable to deal with the external or internal pressures of learning to use the potty. If the condition continues, serious chronic constipation could develop.

training techniques and attitudes, and how your child has responded. This may be a time to revisit your child's signs of readiness or plan a slower approach to toilet training after the constipation has passed. The last thing you want is for your child to develop chronic constipation because you're in a hurry to get him out of diapers.

Sometimes the parents' method of potty training is fine, even low-key, and it's the child who has a type-A personality. Some children push themselves when they are not yet ready. They want to go on the potty so badly, but they just don't have the maturity to make it happen. Other children are so possessive of their BMs that they resist letting them go. Explaining to your child how her body digests and what a BM actually is, and that we all pass BMs again and again, will reassure her. Ask your doctor for advice in your child's particular case. Still, it may be best to stop all training for a while and wait for your child to express interest in starting up again.

Be warned: a certain number of children, for whatever reason, develop a habit of withholding BMs that lasts for years. This problem is far more common than you might think, because parents are reluctant to talk about it or fear that their child might be stigmatized by it. I know of two eight-year-olds who have been on laxatives for years to keep their bowel movements regular and pain free. The parents of these children are still worrying that they somehow created this problem early on by overemphasizing potty training. Just another reason to do yourself (and your child) a favor and go easy on toilet training. Who needs the guilt?

If your child does develop chronic constipation, his doctor may recommend a specialist. Know, too, that withholding BMs may run in families. Ask your own parents if you had this problem.

All about Wiping and Washing

My five-year-old daughter is still very cavalier about wiping, as many kids that age are. I don't think she was aware of the repercussions of hasty (or nonexistent) wiping until I started insisting that she carry her own dirty clothes to the hamper every night. This has given her an awareness of the importance of wiping in a way that I could never have done without using the word "stinky" repeatedly. She can't seem to smell herself but when I see how she carries her underwear two feet in front of her, I have no doubt she'll be a whiz at wiping in no time. In fact she's improved already. It's also wise to review the basics every so often:

- Unroll the toilet paper a few sheets at a time and tear off. (What kid can resist unrolling the whole thing? Why do you think elementary schools have those difficult-to-unroll sheet-by-sheet dispensers?)
- Wipe from front to back.
- Don't stand up and get all the way off the seat while wiping or you'll dribble—onto the floor, into your underpants, down your legs. Try to stay partially seated over the potty.
- Throw toilet paper in the potty. Turn around and make sure that toilet paper has actually made it *into* the potty.
- Flush. (Skip this step if your child is just training and suffers from fear of flushing.)
- Wash hands with soap.
- Dry hands completely.

It never hurts to praise your child for a good cleanup job, especially when he's just catching on. And don't worry about your child making slow progress: Most kids still need help with bathroom hygiene by the time they're six or seven years old. They may even ask you to wipe for them. Instead, let your child do the best he can without help and then do the follow-up wipe. It's also handy to keep moistened wipes near the toilet for really sticky bowel movements. Most novice bathroom goers don't have the patience or skill to dry-wipe a BM.

To encourage hand washing, place a sturdy step stool under the sink and stock the area with fluffy towels. You may want to have a special hand towel and antibacterial soap dispenser (with easy-to-push pump) just for your child. Make sure she knows which spigot is the hot water and that the water can get very hot and burn her. Some parents only let their children wash with cold water until they're five or so. Even then, children can still use cleanup assistance. Don't teach your child how to close the drain (unless you're prepared for an overflowing sink). It's easier to wash under running water. And don't forget to teach your child how to turn *off* the tap.

Getting to the Bathroom on Time

I've seen more than a few parents get pretty angry at their newly potty trained child for not making it to the bathroom on time. Those who were especially peeved had reminded the child to go at a certain time (and he didn't) or suggested that he go before a road trip (and he didn't), and then there was this sudden need to go—and an accident.

Reprimanding a child about potty-related accidents is never going to do much good. It's more productive to say something positive such as, "Whoops. Do you need my help getting cleaned up? I bet you'll make it next time." If you want to help your child remember to go in advance of an outing, enlist his help instead of barking out bathroom orders at him. He'll be more invested in staying dry and visiting the bathroom in time if he's more in control. You might say, "You're in charge of staying dry during our trip to the park tomorrow. I know you can do it. Do you have a plan?" And then help him map out a potty strategy: "Try to go to the bathroom before getting in the car. Take potty in car with us. Locate public restroom at the park." This way he'll know that you're counting on him to stay dry, and he'll have some ideas that you've worked out together for achieving your mutual goal.

Every Child Is Different

During the stage when your child is not making it to the potty every time, remind yourself that she's still learning to understand her body's signals. Bladders come in all sizes and capacities and we each have a different sensitivity level. One child may rush to the potty when she feels the first little urge or twinge; another child may not even notice she has a full bladder until she *really* has to go. And once a child does get on the potty, she has to remember how to release and let go of the urine. That's a lot for a child to master.

My five-year-old still waits until absolutely the last possible minute and then not only does she have to run to the bathroom, she has to use every muscle in her body to keep from having an accident. We're not talking bladder or bowel sphincters here, we're talking about *every* muscle. I've seen her hunch over with her bottom sticking out like a baboon as she shuffles to the bathroom. I've seen her crab-crawl. Sometimes she does a little dance while clutching her vagina. Not once have I seen her walk sedately to the potty. She invariably dribbles and sometimes does more than that. I've asked her why doesn't she just go to the bathroom a little sooner and she says she goes just as soon as her body tells her to.

My older daughter, at that age, never ran to the potty. She just seemed to go when she had to and made sure she was there in time. Her bladder must have had an earlier or more sensitive alarm clock. Children aren't robots, and going to the potty isn't a science. So many things—temperament, bladder size, concentration, and how we tune in to our body's signals—affect each person's ability and style of going to the toilet. And don't forget simple things, such as how much your child drinks. My youngest has always been a thirsty child and drinks three times as much of everything as her older sister. No wonder she's doing the baboon-shuffle to the bathroom.

If you take the time to understand what your child is going through, you'll be less likely to lose your cool about potty mishaps.

Ten Biggest Potty Training Mistakes

Parents want the best for their children, and becoming skilled on the potty seems like such a wonderful accomplishment—of course we want it to happen as smoothly and as soon as possible. But out of eagerness to help our child succeed, we sometimes make mistakes. The great thing about mistakes is our ability to learn from them and here are ten common ones. Avoid them and you'll be well on your way to potty training success. After each mistake is a reminder about the sort of teaching that might be more effective.

1. You start too soon. The opening bell for potty training should sound when your child shows signs of readiness. The date should not be based on the child's age or his birthday or when your older child, the neighbor's child, or your sister's child was trained.

Reminder: Each child has his own timetable. You can begin talking about using the potty well in advance of when you start the actual training. This sort of casual discussion can begin when your child is eighteen months of age or older.

2. *You push too hard.* Parents are sometimes so excited that their child is ready that they overwhelm the child with directions, instructions, commands. Push too hard and your child may rebel.

Reminder: Better to stand back and let your child develop his own potty training style. If you're a card-carrying type A, turn training over to another family member.

3. *Your expectations are too high.* Remind yourself that even though your child is, of course, brilliant, Rome wasn't built in a day. Graduating to the potty won't happen overnight either. Or even in a week or a month.

Reminder: Take it slow and rely on that virtue patience to see you through. Your child has his own timetable. If you follow it, he won't head off to college—or even kindergarten—wearing diapers.

4. *You overpraise.* If you do cartwheels every time your child makes it to the potty, she'll wonder what all the hoopla is about. Maybe she doesn't want to do this potty thing after all.

Reminder: Best to stay casual and matter-of-fact and treat going to the potty for what it is: a natural development that everyone learns at their own pace.

5. *You care too much.* You can't live your child's life for her. Learning to use the potty is your child's achievement, not yours.

Reminder: Your achievement is being savvy enough to follow her cues and give her the help and support she needs. Step back and glow with pride from a safe distance. If you hover, she'll pick up on your anxiety, and it can sabotage her efforts.

6. *You feel competitive about it.* It's hard not to put undue pressure on your child if you're caught up in competing with other parents about who's learning to use the potty first.

Reminder: It's especially counterproductive if you say to your child, "Your friend Sarah is only two and she uses the potty, why don't you want to?" Your child won't understand half of what you said, but she will tune in to your shaming tone. You'll lose the "race" and make your child feel bad.

7. You try to control your child too much. If you're the sort of parent who is hard on yourself, you may find yourself being hard on your child, too. You may want her to do it your way because you think that's the *right* way. You're not alone. Many parents find it hard to just go with the flow and admit that there's more than one right way.

Reminder: Learning to use the toilet, like most developments, is an individual thing that has everything to do with the child's physical, mental, and emotional abilities—and very little to do with what the parent wants.

8. You try to bribe your child. You can't make a child do something she doesn't want to do, or isn't ready to do, so don't go overboard in offering her "incentives."

Reminder: The pleasure of gaining control of her body should be satisfaction (and motivation) enough for your child. If not, see The Pros and Cons of Rewards, page 43. Rewards only work as a little nudge for the child who is ready, but not quite willing.

9. You lose your patience or temper. This potty training business can be trying—for parent and child alike. But if you lose your patience or your temper your child won't learn to use the potty any faster. In fact, it will probably take him longer.

Reminder: Stay cool. If the whole thing is driving you out of your mind, get professional help or take the pressure off of everybody by asking another family member to take over the potty training.

10. You don't have enough faith in your child—or in yourself. Your child will learn to use the potty if you just trust her enough to tell you when she's ready.

Reminder: One of the best things you can do is to show your child that you have faith in her by following her cues and letting her do things her own way. That makes her feel terrific and empowered by the experience of learning to use the potty. She'll feel in charge of what is one of her first achievements of independence.

It's also important to have enough faith in yourself to resist those external pressures that say "you're not training her fast enough or the right way." If you're following your child's lead, you're doing exactly the right thing. Your first true collaborative effort as parent and child (in which your child is an active and willing participant) will be a success.

More power to you—and to your child!

Index

I Can Do It!
HOW I LEARNED TO USE THE POTTY

A Story for Parents and Children

By Anne Krueger
Illustrated by Mary Lynn Blasutta

When I was a baby, Mommy said I did four things *all* the time.

Did you know I filled up a zillion diapers in just one *day*?!

WIPES

That's what babies do, I guess. Babies are *so-o-o* silly.

Now that I'm older I
don't eat mush anymore.
Macaroni and cheese
is my favorite. And
strawberries. Mmmm.

I still go night-night with Bun-Bun and my favorite blankie.

*B*ut now I sleep
all night without
waking up!

***S**ometimes I cry (ouch!).*

But Daddy and Mommy are always there to make me feel better.

And I still pee-pee and poo-poo. But I don't go twenty times a day anymore!

Mommy said that's because
I'm growing up. I don't even
need diapers all the time.

*S*ometimes I wake up in
the morning and I'm dry
all night!

*S*ometimes I wear big-kid pull-on diapers!

Sometimes I run around
in the yard with a bare
bottom! It's really fun!

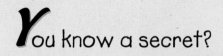You know a secret?

It feels good to be dry.

Mommy and Daddy stay dry all day. They wear underpants and use the bathroom. No diapers for them!

I'll bet I can stay dry too. I would like some underpants of my own.

*L*ast week I got my own little potty!

*I*t's just for me (and Bun-Bun if I say she can use it), and it's just my size.

I like to sit on my potty . Sometimes I sit on it with my clothes on.

*S*ometimes I sit and sit and sit and nothing happens. "That's Okay , " Daddy says. "Try again later."

Do you know what it feels like when you have to go potty? Your tummy starts to feel full or sloshy inside. Sometimes I feel like something's going to come out! That's when I tell Mommy "I gotta go-o-o-o!"

*S*ometimes I'm so busy that I don't make it to the potty in time. "That's Okay," Mommy says. "You're still learning. No big deal."

*I*t's funny when I *do* go in my potty. It makes a funny sound when it lands. Ploooop! Tinkle tinkle!

When we flush it down the big potty it goes "whoooooooosh!" and it takes a ride in the water. "Bye-bye!"

whoooooooosh!

Today I put on my new underpants and took Bun-Bun for a walk in the park.

I pee-peed before we went. I pee-peed when we got back, Bun-Bun said I should be very proud of myself. I am.

Hey, you know what? Mommy was right: Going on the potty is no big deal. I can do it!